Joseph Priestley:
Friends and Foes

As always, to Sarah

Joseph Priestley: Friends and Foes

Remarkable lives in an age of revolution

Keith Baker

Priestley Society

Published by the Priestley Society, UK
(www.priestley.net)

© The Priestley Society 2009

ISBN-10: 0-9558077-1-9 (pb)
ISBN-13: 978-0-9558077-1-8 (pb)

First published 2009

All rights reserved. No part of this publication may be reproduced, stored in a retrieval system, or transmitted, in any form or by any means, electronic, mechanical, photocopying, recording or otherwise, without the prior permission of the publisher.

Copies of this book can be purchased by contacting the Priestley Society c/o:
Stuart Martin (Secretary)
37 Brown Hill Drive, Birkenshaw, Bradford BD11 2AZ, UK
(email: john@martin1364.fsbusiness.co.uk)
or
Keith Baker
75 Hillcote Close, Sheffield S10 3PT, UK
(email: keith.baker3@virgin.net)

Front cover – "Joseph Priestley, the discoverer of oxygen". Painting by Ernest Board by kind permission of the Wellcome Library.
Cover design by Stephen Barlow

Typeset and printed by The Charlesworth Group, Flanshaw Way, Flanshaw Lane, Wakefield WF2 9LP, UK

Contents

List of Illustrations vi
List of Subscribers viii
About the Author ix
Acknowledgements x
Foreword xii

1. Priestley's World 1
2. Benjamin Franklin 14
3. Richard Price 27
4. John Wilkinson 41
5. Anna Barbauld 51
6. Theophilus Lindsey 64
7. Antoine Lavoisier 73
8. Bishop Samuel Horsley 86
9. Thomas Cooper 96
10. King George III, William Pitt and Edmund Burke 108
11. William Cobbett 124
12. The Presidents: George Washington, John Adams and Thomas Jefferson 136
13. Conclusion 156

Notes 166
Further Reading 172
Index 174

List of Illustrations

1. Experiment on a bird in an air pump 2
2. The spread of ideas sometimes fell on deaf ears 4
3. Joseph Priestley as a young man 5
4. Mary Wilkinson 6
5. Lord Shelburne 9
6. The Birmingham mob sets fire to Priestley's home 12
7. The Priestley House in Northumberland, Pennsylvania 13
8. Benjamin Franklin 15
9. John Canton 19
10. A somewhat romantic image of the kite experiment 20
11. Franklin enjoys his popularity with the ladies at the Court of Louis XVI 21
12. Richard Price 27
13. Thomas Bayes 30
14. Price incurs the wrath of both Church and King 37
15. Edmund Burke runs the gauntlet of some contemporary political and literary figures 38
16. John Wilkinson 42
17. One of the few extant buildings associated with the Bersham Ironworks 44
18. Bridge over the River Severn at Coalbrookdale 45
19. John Wilkinson Memorial at Lindale, Cumbria 49
20. Anna Barbauld 51
21. John Aikin, brother to Anna 53
22. A mouse experiment 54
23. Portrait of Anna Barbauld 55
24. Reprint of a page from Barbauld's *Hymns in Prose for Children* 59
25. Theophilus Lindsey 64
26. Priestley, Lindsey and Price campaign for the repeal of the Test and Corporation Acts 67

List of Illustrations

vii

27.	The Essex Street Chapel	68
28.	Lavoisier with his wife Marie-Anne	74
29.	Lavoisier conducts an experiment for visitors with his wife recording	80
30.	Priestley and Lavoisier, church minister and aristocrat	82
31.	Samuel Horsley	86
32.	Joseph Banks, President of the Royal Society	88
33.	Thomas Cooper	96
34.	An early view of Northumberland on the Susquehanna River	101
35.	Dickinson College	105
36.	Thomas Cooper in later life	106
37.	King George III, William Pitt and Edmund Burke	108
38.	Gillray cartoon of Priestley calling for the head of George III	111
39.	Doctor Phlogiston or Political Priest	111
40.	George III as a huntsman holding Napoleon's head	112
41.	Two men arguing over the Test laws	114
42.	Storming of the Bastille	115
43.	William Pitt on the search for revolutionaries	117
44.	Pitt steering a boat, *The Constitution*	118
45.	Frontispiece to Burke's *Reflections*	120
46.	Cartoon showing Edmund Burke as Don Quixote	122
47.	William Cobbett	124
48.	Cobbett – Ploughboy to Army	126
49.	Peter Porcupine – Cobbett as editor	130
50.	Cobbett as an MP	134
51.	George Washington	137
52.	Washington resigns his commission as Commander-in-Chief	138
53.	Dinner at Mount Vernon	139
54.	John Adams	141
55.	Abigail Adams	143
56.	Peacefield	145
57.	Thomas Jefferson	149
58.	The Louisiana Purchase	151
59.	Monticello	152
60.	An early representation of the American Dream	164

List of Subscribers

Sponsors
Alan Dronsfield Trust
Leeds Philosophical and Literary Society

Subscribers	Affiliation
Ian & Kate Abley	Abacus
Dorothy Archer	National Unitarian Fellowship
Bill Bailey	Woodkirk Specialist Science School
Batley Grammar School	
Jim & Lesley Birch	Priestley Society
Jerome David Bowers	North Illinois University USA
Malcolm Byard	Priestley Society
Richard Crossley	University of York
Peter Excell	Glyndwr University Wrexham
Vladimir Gorelov	Elland
Paul Goulden	Priestley Society
Mike Hanson	Roberttown
Edward & Margaret Hill	Belper
Carol & William Hoover	Ruby Valley Research Institute USA
Graham Kingsley	Baldock
Joe Lee	Priestley Society
Stuart Martin	Priestley Society
Colin Moore	Rotary Club of Headingley
Paul Neaves	Star Centre USA
John Norman	University of Sheffield
Roy Olofson	PA State University USA
Ann Peart	Unitarian College Manchester
Suzanne Priestley	Priestley Society
David Richardson	Priestley Family USA
Glen Rodgers	Loudon USA
Norman Rose	University of Birmingham
John Rowlinson	University of Oxford
Kate Taylor	Westgate Chapel, Wakefield
Priestley Toulmin	Priestley Family USA

Geoff Turton	Leeds
Margaret Ware	Priestley Family
Ruth Watts	University of Birmingham
Randy Wayne	Cornell University USA
Leslie Woodcock	Priestley Society
Raymond Woodcock	Old Batelians
Christopher Wooller	Heckmondwike & District Rotary Club
David Zuck	History of Anaesthesia Society

About the Author

Keith Baker is a writer and former civil servant whose interest in Priestley and his circle first began when he was a governor of the Joseph Priestley College in Leeds, UK.

Acknowledgements

The idea for this book came from the time when I was a governor of the Joseph Priestley College in Leeds, UK, so my thanks first must be to the College for arousing my interest in the life of Joseph Priestley and his friends and foes.

I am also very grateful to the other institutions which enabled me to carry out the research for the book. I am fortunate enough to live not far from the British Library at Boston Spa, Yorkshire, and so was able to draw extensively on the excellent stock of books and periodicals housed there. Similarly, I am grateful for access to, and use of, material held at Warrington Local Studies Library, the John Rylands Library at Manchester, the Dr Williams' Library in London and the Sheffield University Library. My numerous requests and queries to staff at these libraries were always dealt with efficiently and helpfully and I wish to extend my sincere thanks to them.

As indicated by my references and the further reading, I have relied heavily on the researches, books and articles of many scholars whose knowledge of the people portrayed in this book greatly exceeds my own. Any errors of fact or of interpretation I have made are entirely mine, and I apologise if I have inadvertently infringed any copyright.

This book would not have been published without the generous assistance of the Priestley Society based in Heckmondwike, Yorkshire. Under the enthusiastic Chairmanship of Professor Woodcock, the Society does much to encourage world-wide interest and research into Priestley's life and achievements. I have personally benefited greatly from the help and encouragement of several of the Society's members during the lengthy writing of this book. Special thanks are due to Dr Joe Lee whose kind and meticulous reading of the initial draft prevented many errors and infelicities; to Stephen Barlow, the gifted designer of the book cover, and to Henry Stokeley, the Society's skilful webmaster.

The American interest is a strong theme of the book and I thank Professor J.D. Bowers, Professor of History at Northern Illinois University, for reading the manuscript and for providing such a perceptive Foreword. I am grateful, too, to Dr Malcolm Dick at the University of Birmingham for his constructive comments on early parts of the book.

For the printing and marketing of the book, I am much indebted to the knowledge and expertise of staff of the Charlesworth Group in Wakefield, UK, and especially to Caitlin Meadows, Publishing Services Director, and Dawn Beaumont and Noel Sadler, whose many helpful suggestions and thoughtfulness have proved invaluable.

I should like also to acknowledge the generous financial assistance provided to me by the Leeds Philosophical and Literary Society, and the personal contribution of Professor Dronsfield, Chair of the Historical Group, Royal Society of Chemistry.

Finally, my greatest debt is to my wife Sarah who has been throughout my most important reader, critic and supporter. And also for her forbearance and patience at times when it must have seemed that the friends and foes of Joseph Priestley had long outstayed their welcome in our household.

Foreword

Joseph Priestley was a man of singular importance and great accomplishment. His achievements in the fields of religion, science, politics and education endure to this very day. Indeed, he, like Jefferson and many other contemporaries, was a renaissance man. But one cannot be so successful without meaningful and substantial contributions from one's friends and associates. Those who joined with Priestley in his religious pursuits, aided him in his scientific experiments, funded his ventures and supported his views were instrumental in his success.

With such far-reaching interests and accomplishments, however, came many opponents. There were those who challenged and rejected Priestley's ideas, beliefs and results, calling him a heretic and a hack. Their opposition forced Priestley to reproduce his experiments and defend his views. Indeed, a great portion of Priestley's written corpus consists of tracts and papers attacking his opponents and responding to their critiques.

In short, Joseph Priestley was indeed a man who was defined by both friend and foe.

In this solidly written work, Keith Baker introduces us to this essential facet of Priestley's life and in so doing brings many other aspects of Priestley and his achievements into focus. By examining those who crossed Priestley's path, sometimes permanently and other times much more fleetingly, this work allows the reader to understand and appreciate the life and thoughts of Priestley and to contemplate his personal world on a more fundamental and much deeper level. We are able to see the virtues of dissent that Priestley cherished even as they tore at his personal views and we can better consider the transatlantic and global society in which he existed as he (along with most of his family) and his ideas crossed and re-crossed politically imposed and natural boundaries. Priestley valued, greatly, the search for truth in all matters religious, social and political. By showing us how Priestley drew inspiration from his close associates and used the arguments of his opponents to hone his own ideas for both elucidation and argumentation, we can see how this quest for truth was dualistic in nature and the intellectual ties that bound him to his supporters and detractors, as well as the extent to which his ideas transcended any one discipline.

Priestley lived in a time quite unlike any other and yet one that has remarkable similarities to our own. He lived at a time when revolutions – of thought, government, industry and identity – were seemingly innocent and yet they fundamentally changed the world. In this book, then, Baker plants the seeds for further inquiry and new investigations. *Joseph Priestley: Friends and Foes* is then an excellent contribution to our understanding of who Joseph Priestley was in his own day. Each of the chapters herein examines this dual dimension of Priestley's life and associations; but it is about more than just the concepts of friendship and opposition (dare I say hatred in a few cases), although those are judiciously explored and employed within these chapters. In fact, the book allows anyone interested in Priestley to explore how familial ties shaped Priestley, how his ideas were a catalyst to friendships that would last a lifetime and how his response to his opponents also created some of his most important and lasting contributions. Thus Baker answers many questions about Priestley and his world, but also leads us to ask new ones as we seek greater understanding and meaning from the life of one of history's most revered and accomplished men.

J.D. Bowers
Northern Illinois University
DeKalb, Illinois, USA

CHAPTER 1

Priestley's World

Those delving into the life and times of Joseph Priestley would be struck by two thoughts. First, the sheer variety of his interests spanning the worlds of science, theology, education and political reform, and the energy, determination and courage bordering on recklessness with which he pursued them. One historian has referred to him as *"a polymath born with a perpetual motion pen"*.[1] And, secondly, his relationships with a large number of remarkable and fascinating people whose lives and fortunes at one time or another became inextricably linked with his own. Amongst them were very close friends of Priestley but he also made some powerful and implacable enemies.

The main purpose of this book is to introduce the interested reader to a group of these exceptional people, both friends and foes, and to examine how they interacted during their lives with Priestley. Given the scope and achievements of Priestley's life, selecting any such list is bound to be a somewhat arbitrary and contentious exercise, and I am conscious that there are many others who could well have been included. For example, his eminent friends in the Lunar Society, notably James Watt, Josiah Wedgwood and Matthew Boulton, have a particularly strong case for inclusion but their association with Priestley has been admirably covered elsewhere in several publications, especially in the book by Jenny Uglow.[2]

All the characters in the book lived and worked during the age of the Enlightenment of the eighteenth century, the century called by the French the "*siècle des lumières*" – the century of light – because of its emphasis on reason as the basis of authority and the opening up of knowledge. They were turbulent and momentous years, and all our characters contributed significantly in one way or another to the important developments then taking place in many different fields of human endeavour. To place our portraits in context therefore, we need to describe some of the major characteristics of the times.

The Enlightenment in Britain
In some respects it was an Augustan age. Through costly but successful wars, Britain had emerged from a relatively small maritime state into a very powerful one with a large empire on which the sun never set. Some of its greatest statesmen, orators, generals, artists and historians flourished during this period. It might still be governed by a political establishment drawn mainly from the

aristocracy, the landed gentry and the established Church, but they presided over a country in which far-reaching economic, religious, scientific, social and political developments were taking place.

The population of England and Wales was increasing rapidly. By 1770 it had reached over seven million. The Industrial Revolution was gathering momentum and bringing changes not only in manufacturing, transport and commerce, but in society generally. Large numbers of poor agricultural labourers suffered from the notorious Enclosure Acts. With the growth of the towns, a new middle class of traders and businessmen was emerging, less dependent on church and squire. Britain was breaking free from the past and moving irrevocably from an agricultural, household economy to an industrial based economy, and in the process not without some violence.

The Enlightenment fed a new confidence in the future amongst the middle classes. People like Priestley and his friends were convinced that past errors could be corrected by the use of reason, and that civil and political equality was at last in their grasp. The Scientific Revolution flourished; great discoveries were being made in the fields of medicine, electricity and chemistry that were to have an enormous impact on the face of the world and the lives of ordinary people. In

1. Experiment on a Bird in an Air Pump 1768. Painting by Joseph Wright of Derby. A crowd watches an early experiment into the nature of air and its ability to support life

1780 Benjamin Franklin wrote to his friend Joseph Priestley saying he regretted sometimes the fact that he had been born too soon, and speculating that it was *"impossible to imagine the height to which may be carried, in a thousand years, the power of man over matter"*.

Historic political revolutions were taking place across the world. The American War and the Declaration of Independence had a crucial influence on the radicalisation of Britain. The freedom and rights enjoyed by the new nation were greeted by reformers as heralding a fresh era in the history of mankind and a time to begin anew. No wonder, prophesied the poet William Blake, *"The King of England looking westwards trembles at the vision"*.[3] As we shall see, several people in this study identified America with the future of Britain. But the greatest impact of all on late eighteenth century Britain came from the French Revolution. It shook society to its very depths. Welcomed with joy by liberals as the birth of equality and liberty, it was soon feared and condemned by many as the most dangerous enemy that ever disturbed the peace of the world. John Wesley saw it as the work of Satan. The fires lit by the Revolution inflamed the British domestic scene and embroiled Britain in a war lasting a decade.

Domestic affairs were also under strain from another source. The 1760s saw mounting criticism of the established social and political order and the very institutions of English life. There was agitation to extend the suffrage and to redistribute parliamentary representation. Critics no longer regarded the constitution and all the apparatus of the state as a defence against repression, but more as restrictions on personal and civil freedoms. In the latter part of the eighteenth century the repeal of the Test and Corporation Acts became the main political objective of the Dissenters who were excluded by the Acts from all branches of civil government and from holding political office.

Prominent in the reform movement were the so-called Rational Dissenters, the group of liberal intellectuals like Priestley who were drawn from the middle ranks of English society and with good connections with business and commerce. They were strongly established in the growing towns. Earnest, well educated and in touch with the spirit of the times, they did not draw back from leading the campaign for reform. *"I bless God"* said Priestley, *"that I was born a Dissenter, not manacled by the chains of so debasing a system as that of the Church of England, and that I was not educated at Oxford or Cambridge"*.[4] However, on three successive occasions – March 1787, May 1789 and March 1790 – the Rational Dissenters headed by Priestley failed in their efforts to repeal the Test and Corporation Acts. Similarly little progress was made in social and parliamentary reform.

The natural allies of the political reformers were religious groups campaigning for an enlargement of their own liberties. Influenced by the Enlightenment, religion had become more a matter of personal reason and choice. By continental standards, religious freedom was widespread. The country abounded with so many new sects, frequently branded as heretical, that an explanatory dictionary had to be published. Some Presbyterians were drawn towards becoming Unitarians, who along with the Roman Catholics and non-Christians (mostly Jews) did not officially enjoy rights of public worship under the Toleration Act of 1689. Nor was the Church of England itself immune from internal tensions. There were pressures for reform from the Methodist revival and a growing hostility among the Anglican clergy to what some saw as the tyranny of the Thirty-Nine Articles of Religion.

In poetry and literature one can discern the beginnings of the Romantic Movement. There was a reaction against past conventions with its emphasis on form and narrow themes, and a consequent move to writing that reflected more of the language of the heart. The human condition, childhood, love and death, a person's relation to nature, all emerged as acceptable and popular themes. The growth of a reading public and the massive expansion of the printing and publishing industry gave an enormous boost to the spread of knowledge, news and radical views. Printed material abounded on everything under the sun, including caricature. Numerous journals, especially scientific, were launched. The first real children's books appeared. Political and religious pamphleteers and propagandists, including for the first time women, exploited the opportunity to express their views on public and political matters. It was, said Samuel Johnson, *"the Age of Authors"*.

2. The spread of ideas sometimes fell on deaf ears

Such mighty changes had a deep influence on the lives of the people who appear in the pages which follow and perhaps none more so than on Joseph Priestley himself. By sketching the life of this remarkable man we can, in the process, introduce to the reader the people – his friends and foes – whom we shall be featuring in the book.

Joseph Priestley
Joseph Priestley was born in 1733 at Birstall Fieldhead, a small hamlet in the West Riding of Yorkshire, near Leeds. He was the son of a poor Yorkshire cloth-dresser and had an unsettled childhood. His mother died early and at the age of nine he was adopted by his aunt, Sarah Keighley. A Presbyterian, she brought Priestley up as a strict Calvinist but she was no bigot and ensured that he had a good education. Intellectually very bright, he had a natural gift for languages. He left Batley Grammar School at the age of 16, by which time he had learned Hebrew, Latin and Greek, as well as several modern languages. He was destined for the Presbyterian ministry and in 1752 he entered the Dissenting Academy at Daventry. Since Dissenters were debarred from attending Oxford or Cambridge, they had set up their own academies which proved significantly superior to the older universities. As well as religion, they taught history, modern languages, science and economics, and approached all subjects with a critical rather than a reverential eye. It was an environment in which the

3. Joseph Priestley as a young man

young Priestley flourished since he had developed an intense distaste for dogma of any source. Whilst at Daventry he became convinced that the career of a religious minister was the noblest of all professions, a conviction from which, despite all his other achievements he never departed, and which had a huge influence on all his life and work.

On leaving Daventry in 1755 he became a minister to a Dissenting congregation at Needham Market in Suffolk, with a salary of £30 a year. He felt isolated and lonely and was not a success. The congregation did not approve of his leaning towards Arian theology which denied the complete divinity of Jesus and gave primacy to God the Father. He also was badly distressed by a speech impediment which was made better only by a course of treatment in London paid for by his aunt. He left for another more liberal congregation in Nantwich, Cheshire in 1758, where he supplemented his meagre salary with some teaching. The reputation he soon established as a good teacher led to an invitation in 1761 to become a "Tutor of Languages" at the new Dissenting Academy at Warrington, then in Lancashire.

The Academy at Warrington was to become the most illustrious of all the Dissenting Academies and had a great deal of influence on Priestley's future career. Whilst at the Academy he was awarded the degree of Doctor of Law by the University of Edinburgh for his *Chart of Biography* (1764). Never one to be restricted, he soon branched out into several fields of study, including chemistry and the new science of electricity, and built himself a small laboratory. His interests soon brought him into contact with members of the dissenting elite and with other eminent scientists and philosophers. From Warrington he made frequent visits to London in order to supplement his knowledge. It was there in 1765 that he met the two friends who were to play a vital role in helping him embark upon his scientific career. They were the famous American, **Benjamin Franklin** (Chapter 2), then in England as representative of the Pennsylvania government, and **Richard Price** (Chapter 3), the eminent philosopher, theologian and statistician, and a pioneer of the insurance industry.

Soon after moving to Warrington, Priestley married Mary Wilkinson in 1762 whom Priestley described as *"a women of excellent understanding, much improved by reading, of great fortitude and strength of mind, and of a temper in the highest degree affectionate and generous"*. Although Priestley was devoted to his work, he was always prepared to set aside two or three hours a day to games such as cards and backgammon, but particularly chess which he and his wife played regularly every evening. Mary was the daughter of Isaac Wilkinson and sister to John and William Wilkinson. Both the brothers became friends of Priestley but it was his friendship with **John Wilkinson** (Chapter 4), which was by far the most significant. John became the greatest and most eccentric of all the early iron masters, and was an important benefactor and supporter of the Priestley family.

4. Mary Wilkinson. Very intelligent and original, her letters tended to be rather brighter than those written by Priestley

At Warrington, Priestley also met Anna Aikin, the bright and lively daughter of John Aikin who was a fellow teacher at Warrington. Priestley encouraged Anna to write verse. Later as **Mrs Anna Barbauld** (Chapter 5), she became a popular writer, critic and poet of her time, and is now appreciated as an accomplished literary figure of the late eighteenth century. Anna formed a close and life-long friendship with the Priestley family, and especially with Mary Priestley, but Anna by no means accepted all of Joseph's views during her lifetime.

With enthusiastic support from his friends Benjamin Franklin and Richard Price, Joseph Priestley was elected in 1766 to the Royal Society at the relatively young age of 33, largely as a consequence of his experimental work on electricity. In the following year, Priestley published the results of his experiments in his first major scientific work *The History and Present State of Electricity*. The book was an immediate success and was built around his theory that the history of science was important because it showed how human intelligence could learn directly from the forces of nature to promote progress.

Although Priestley was happy at Warrington, by 1767 his wife Mary had become concerned about what she considered to be the unhealthy air of the Mersey, and the Academy also had financial problems. They now had a daughter, Sally, and Priestley, conscious of his family responsibilities, was persuaded to take a better paid post as a minister at the Mill Hill Chapel (or Meeting House as it was called in Priestley's time) in Leeds. The Priestleys were at home in this growing, bustling town and two sons were born to them there – Joseph junior and William. Priestley was pleased to minister to such *"a liberal, friendly and harmonious congregation"*, and he served them well; in addition to his ministerial duties, as secretary of the organising committee, he mustered enough support to establish in Leeds one of the first successful public-subscription libraries in England.

It was at Leeds that he first publicly declared his religious views when he published his *Institutes of Natural and Revealed Religion*. This work, the first volume of which was published in 1769, made a powerful contribution to the development of the Unitarian movement. It also shocked many readers and instantly provoked the hostility of the Church of England and King George III. Although Priestley believed Jesus to be an inspired man and a great religious teacher, he had now moved to the full Unitarian position and rejected Christ's divinity. In his *Institutes*, Priestley whilst believing in a Christian God, argued that all the trappings of Christianity – the deification and worship of Jesus and the Virgin Mary, the doctrine of the Trinity and *"of innumerable other saints, and of angels also"* – were simply corruptions of Jesus's early teaching which had been made by the early Church in its struggle for ascendancy.

Theological works might have been his priority but Priestley did not neglect his scientific work. It was at Leeds that his genius as an experimental chemist began to flourish. He made several important discoveries, particularly those associated with the nature and properties of gases. In all, he is credited with the discovery of nine previously unknown gases. In a matter of a few years he established an international reputation and decided to embark on a very ambitious plan to write a history of the whole of experimental philosophy. To obtain all the books and resources required for such a study and to carry out further experiments, Priestley sought all the help he could get from his friends and acquaintances. It was at Leeds where Priestley made the acquaintance of an Anglican clergyman, **Theophilus Lindsey** (Chapter 6), a rector at Catterick, Yorkshire. Lindsey was socially well connected and proved to be helpful in getting him the support of wealthy patrons such as the Duke of Northumberland. This was the start of a most productive and long lasting friendship between the two men. Lindsey was eventually to resign from the Church of England and become the minister of the first avowedly Unitarian Chapel in England, on Essex Street off the Strand in London.

Increasingly, Priestley found himself drawn into political philosophy stimulated by the ideas of the radical circle of friends he was meeting in London. In 1768 he published his *Essay on the First Principles of Government*. In this work he argued for a political system that maximised human liberty and the right of an oppressed people to rebel against a tyrannical ruler. A year later he further developed his ideas in his work on *The State of Public Liberty*. These books, together with his attack on the British government for restricting the rights and liberties of the American colonists, further antagonised conservative opinion.

Priestley and his family had no wish to leave Leeds, but in 1772 he received an offer from the Earl of Shelburne, a prominent Whig politician with reformist views, to become his *Librarian and Literary Companion*. Shelburne had a genuine interest in Priestley's scientific work, and the offer made was a generous one – twice his present salary, a house on the Earl's estate at Bowood House, near Calne in Wiltshire, another in London, funds for his experiments and the use of the magnificent library at Bowood. With some reluctance the Priestleys agreed to the move. Shelburne lived up to his word and proved to be a supportive and generous patron, and it was in his service that Priestley made further scientific discoveries that astonished the scientific world. As well as the process of photosynthesis, he identified gases such as sulphur dioxide, nitrous oxide, nitric oxide but the greatest of all was the discovery of the gas he called *"dephlogisticated air"* or oxygen as it was later named. It was during his time with Lord Shelburne that Priestley also wrote most of his important philosophical works.

In the autumn of 1774 Priestley joined Shelburne on a tour of the European continent where he took the opportunity of meeting several philosophers and scientists. Before returning home, he spent some time in Paris where he demonstrated some of his experiments. It was during one particularly lavish dinner in

5. Lord Shelburne. Although unpopular with his peers, he was regarded with respect and affection by radicals and Dissenters such as Price and Priestley

October 1774, hosted by the brilliant French aristocrat and scientist, **Antoine Lavoisier** (Chapter 7), at which Priestley famously described to the assembled company his discovery of his dephlogisticated air. As we shall later see, this occasion marked the beginning of the long and bitter rivalry between the two scientists over the discovery of oxygen and the development of chemistry.

When the Priestleys' third son was born in 1777 they named him Henry at Lord Shelburne's request. However, by 1780 the working relationship between Shelburne and Priestley had cooled; perhaps even this liberal politician became nervous of some of his protégé's more outspoken political and religious views. Priestley decided to move to Birmingham with his family where he soon took up a preaching post at the new Meeting House. Since this was one of the most liberal congregations in England, it was an appointment much to his liking and in many ways this was the happiest period of his life. He was also delighted to be able to join the famous Lunar Society, that small but hugely influential group of academics, scientists and industrialists who met monthly and whose ideas and work helped establish the Industrial Revolution in Britain. Among his friends were Matthew Boulton, the pioneering industrialist and his partner, James Watt of the steam engine; Josiah Wedgwood, the famous potter; and Erasmus Darwin, doctor, inventor, poet and grandfather of Charles Darwin. Living as he did in the burgeoning industrial heartland of England, Priestley could apply some of his discoveries to practical problems encountered by prominent Midland industrialists, and particularly those of his brother-in-law John Wilkinson.

His religious and scientific work proceeded hand in hand. He persisted with his outspoken criticism of the established church. Not surprisingly, religious and political leaders grew ever more alarmed by the radical views which he expressed in elaborate and important books such as *The History of the Corruptions of Christianity* (1782) and *History of Early Opinions concerning Jesus Christ* (1786), which challenged head-on basic Christian orthodoxies. Priestley was denounced from the pulpit and in the House of Commons as an agent of Satan. In defence of the established church leapt the powerful Archdeacon of St Albans, **Samuel Horsley** (Chapter 8), reputed to be the ablest Anglican cleric of his time. His public dispute with Priestley during the 1780s was regarded as the fiercest and most bitter religious controversy of the age.

Nor did Priestley neglect his work for political reform. He actively championed the Dissenters' Parliamentary campaign to repeal the Test and Corporation Acts, and the need to disestablish the Church of England. His opponents responded with accusations that his real purposes were more sinister – not only to overthrow the Church of England but the King along with much of the apparatus of the State as well. Not for the first or last time, his impassioned public comments played into the hands of his enemies. In a sermon on Guy Fawkes Day in 1785 he delivered a sermon using the word "*revolution*" three times in describing the fall of the Roman Empire, and then depicting the Dissenters as *"laying gunpowder, grain by grain, under the old building of error and superstition, which a single spark may hereafter inflame, so as to produce an instantaneous explosion"*. His enemies seized upon the words to confirm Priestley as a very dangerous agitator and to stigmatise him as *"Gunpowder Jo"*.

Political and religious tensions were inflamed by the outbreak of the French Revolution in 1789. Priestley and his friends welcomed it as a force for good and an opportunity to promote universal peace and goodwill among nations. On receiving the news of the fall of the Bastille, Priestley's youngest son Harry could not contain his excitement, rushing to and fro and crying out *"Hurrah! Liberty, Reason, brotherly love for ever! Down with kingcraft and priest craft"*. And Wordsworth wrote *"Bliss was it in that dawn to be alive"*. But in a matter of months fears arose in conservative circles that civil strife and revolution might well spread to Britain. Nor were King George III and his supporters pleased to learn Joseph's Priestley's prediction that the Revolution also meant that monarchs will be the *"first servants of the people and accountable to them"*.

Unwisely, Priestley set about establishing in Birmingham a radical Constitutional Society similar to that in Manchester which had already attracted the suspicions of the authorities. One of those he consulted was his young radical friend, the chemist, **Thomas Cooper** (Chapter 9), who was destined to play an influential part in Priestley's emigration to America. The two men subsequently settled close together in America where they continued to co-operate on scientific and politically matters, not always in Priestley's best interests. Cooper later made important contributions to the public life of early nineteenth century America.

As the French Revolution degenerated into violence and bloodshed, the fears of revolution in Britain and invasion from France were intensified. The propertied class took fright and a conservative reaction set in. These were dangerous times for any opponents of the government. By 1792 **King George III** (Chapter 10) and his able but haughty Prime Minister, **William Pitt** (Chapter 10) had become convinced that stringent steps were needed to curb the activities of radicals and agitators like Priestley. The government introduced repressive legislation, a measure that drew powerful support from the important conservative political writer and thinker, **Edmund Burke** (Chapter 10). Burke had earlier published in 1790 his influential work, *Reflections on the Revolution in France*, which had condemned those who supported the Revolution, and he now followed this up with a relentless public campaign against the Dissenters and their leaders Priestley and Price.

Priestley characteristically ignored the attacks upon him and pressed on with his demands for reform. Events took a much more violent turn when the pro-Revolution Constitutional Society in Birmingham organised a dinner on 14 July 1791 to commemorate the storming of the Bastille. Although Priestley did not

6. The Birmingham mob sets fire to Priestley's home

attend the dinner, the Tories in the city made inflammatory speeches attacking Priestley's political views. Riots broke out, and a large drunken mob chanting "*Down with Priestley*" stormed and burned the homes of prominent merchants and manufacturers in the city and its Dissenting Chapels. The mob broke into Priestley's house, setting it on fire and destroying his books, papers and scientific apparatus. When dawn broke the surrounding fields were strewn with prostrate figures sleeping from fatigue and drunkenness.

Priestley and his family were lucky to escape with their lives. He fled with his family to London and taught history and science for a while at the New College in Hackney. His personal situation was not enhanced by the act of the French National Convention in September 1792 honouring him with French citizenship. He continued to be persecuted for his political and religious beliefs and he feared for the safety of his family. He was burned in effigy along with the radical Thomas Paine. Unhappily, too, he was shunned by many of his former friends. His two eldest sons had left England for America, and in 1794 Joseph and Mary decided that they too would emigrate to the new Republic. They were joined by their youngest son, Henry, but their married daughter, Sally, stayed with her family in England.

On arrival in America Priestley was given a warm welcome by his admirers, amongst whom was the first President, **George Washington** (Chapter 12). He soon settled with his family in Northumberland, Pennsylvania, very near an area of land earmarked for British and other emigrés seeking political and religious freedom. However his final years were far from happy ones. His favourite son, Henry, died in 1795 and his beloved wife, Mary, a year later. He felt cut off and

7. The Priestley Home in Northumberland, Pennsylvania. The house was designed by Mary, Priestley's wife, and completed in 1798

greatly missed his friends. His efforts to establish a permanent English Unitarian congregation proved very difficult and only the Universalists in Philadelphia permitted him to preach regularly from their pulpit. He was surprised and dismayed too at the political intolerance which he encountered in the New World. Virtually from his arrival in New York, he was hounded in the press by the vitriolic pen of another English refugee, the fiery young journalist, **William Cobbett** (Chapter 11), who wrote under the pseudonym *"Peter Porcupine"*.

Unwisely, Priestley allowed himself to be dragged into American politics which were particularly stormy at the time. His differences with **John Adams** (Chapter 12), the second President of the United States, fractured their former friendship, so much so that he was in grave danger of deportation. Only when **Thomas Jefferson** (Chapter 12), a fervent admirer of Priestley, became President in 1801 did Priestley fully enjoy the peace and security he had hoped for in the New World.

Soon after 1803 Joseph Priestley's health went into decline, describing himself as an *"exhausted volcano"*. He died at his home in Northumberland on 6 February 1804, aged 71, working to the last on his annotations of the Old and New Testaments. His friend Thomas Cooper was with him. Priestley was heard to remark to all those gathered around him of the peculiarly happy situation the Divine Being had placed him in life, and *"the great advantage he had enjoyed in the acquaintance and friendship of some of the best and wisest men in the age in which he had lived"*.[5]

CHAPTER 2

Benjamin Franklin
(1706–1790)
The Great American

The fifteenth child of a Boston candle-maker, Benjamin Franklin became one of the most famous Americans of his time. Statesman, journalist, humorist, inventor and scientist, he was a foremost leader of the Enlightenment and won the recognition of scientists and intellectuals across Europe. He helped shape the American Revolution, and was the only one who was a signatory to all three founding documents of the new Republic – the Declaration of Independence, the Peace Treaty with Great Britain and the American Constitution. Although no American state is named after him, (Tennessee tried hard to do so), almost every other type of American institution has been – towns, schools, colleges, hospitals and many children too. He was 30 years older than Joseph Priestley, and, as we shall see, a very different character. Nonetheless, he became the first important patron of Priestley, his mentor and a close and influential friend.

Franklin had an exceptionally creative and ingenious mind. He was born curious. Even in the years when he was heavily engaged on important political and diplomatic assignments, his restless mind could turn to more mundane projects such as how to deal with smoking chimneys, cleaning streets, draining swamps or improving water troughs for horses. In his early years, there was something of the 'smart alec' about him but he was simply testing his powers; he quickly learned that ridicule and scoring points convinced no one, lost friends and made enemies. He developed "*the habit of expressing myself in terms in terms of modest diffidence*", and in time this became his natural style.[1] Priestley noted that strangers sometimes found Franklin too reserved and lacking in emotion. On first acquaintance, he was no 'hail fellow well met', but throughout his life he showed a remarkable interest in people of all ages, sorts and backgrounds. Once people got to know him they became charmed by his manners and the generosity of his character. As a result he made friends in many lands, and for the most part kept them.

He was a great exponent of self improvement. A close observer of his own times, he analysed carefully what useful lessons could be drawn from successes and failures, including his own. An accomplished writer, his works are full of prudent hints on how to overcome problems in life and to survive in a world full of deception and folly. His famous book entitled *Poor Richard's Almanac* is aimed at improving public attitudes and behaviour. It is made up numerous maxims for success in life and the value of work, such as:

> *The wise man proceeds cautiously, keeps his own council, and guards his tongue;*
> *Half a truth is often a great lie;*
> *Little strokes fell great oaks;*
> *Beware of little expenses, a small leak will sink a ship;*
> *He that riseth late must trot all day;*
> *There are three fruitful friends, an old wife, an old dog, and ready money.*[2]

For some, Franklin's apparent high mindedness and ceaseless efforts to do good have simply been too much. It was once said that his moralising *"established a rock of philosophic materialism against which generations of sensitive craft beat in vain"*.[3] Mark Twain was another who admired Franklin's technological genius, but his apparent pleasure in work, his desire to get things done and tell the world of his achievements were to Twain simply a screen for ideas and conduct calculated to make miserable the lives of boys *"who might*

8. Benjamin Franklin

otherwise have been happy".[4] Another critic was the writer, D.H. Lawrence, who considered that Franklin was very wrong about the perfectibility of man, and depicted Franklin as a *"snuff-coloured little man, a bourgeois, self-satisfied man and a threat to the imagination and the spirit"*.[5]

However, *Poor Richard's Almanac* was undoubtedly popular and read widely throughout the American colonies and reprinted in many editions abroad. Its gospel was particularly attractive to small tradesmen and businessmen on the make. Franklin provided them with just the home-spun philosophy they wanted and they took to its maxims avidly. That does not mean that Franklin necessarily always practised what he preached. In fact, once he had established his own business interests, he was quite prepared to change his habits and opinions, and readily mingle with the leisured classes. In his later years the man who had earlier preached *"Early to bed, early to rise"* rarely rose before ten o'clock.[6] He became in fact well-known for his love of pleasure, company, a laugh and a glass of wine, and to his enemies he lived a dissolute life, very far from *"the tight little defender of the middle-class world"*.[7]

His attitude to religion was complex and his remarks on God, religion and ethics could be baffling. He refused to endorse any particular religious doctrine, believing that they all shared common virtues. Some people saw him as an unorthodox Christian far ahead of his time. Others condemned him as an infidel, and hostile to any religious sentiments; his colleague John Adams (Chapter 12) sneered that he belonged to the ranks of *"Atheists, Deists and Libertines"*. Priestley, who knew him better than most, grudgingly allowed that Franklin did believe in the existence of a God. But he deplored the fact that a man of his great influence should have been an unbeliever in Christianity, and who had *"also done so much as he did to make others non believers"*.[8] Priestley took pains to give his friend religious books to study but without much success. However, it is fair to say in so far as Franklin had religious beliefs, they were probably closest to the Unitarian position than others. Shortly before his death he admitted that the system of morals and religion left by Jesus of Nazareth was *"the best the world ever saw or is like to see; but I apprehend it has received various corrupting changes, and I have, with most of the present Dissenters in England, some doubts as to his divinity"*.[9]

Early Life
Franklin was born in Boston, Massachusetts in 1706. His father, who was a maker of candles and soap, married twice and fathered 17 children. Benjamin was the youngest son. Although his parents talked of a career in the church for him, his schooling ended when he was 10 and he worked for his father for a short time. At the age of 12 he became an apprentice to his brother James who created the *New England Courant*, the first truly independent paper in the American colonies. Benjamin wanted to write for the paper but his brother

would not let him, so he began writing letters by night under the pseudonym of *Mrs Silence Dogwood* which he then had printed and sneaked into the paper. The letters were a great success and before long everyone wanted to know who the real Silence Dogwood was. When Benjamin confessed that he had been writing the letters, his brother became jealous, even beating him from time to time. Eventually he had had enough, and at the age of 17 he ran away to Philadelphia.

There he found work as an apprentice printer. He did so well that the Governor of Pennsylvania, Sir William Keith, promised to set him up in business if he went to London to buy some printing equipment. However, the Governor reneged on his promise and Ben was forced to spend several months in London doing print work. He eventually returned to Philadelphia in 1726, and by 1730 had set up a printing house of his own, and began publishing *The Pennsylvania Gazette*.

In the same year he asked his childhood sweetheart, Deborah Read, to marry him. She was very fond of Benjamin but whilst Franklin was in London she had made an unfortunate marriage to a man called John Rogers who later fled to Barbados to escape prosecution for his debts. There were also rumours that he already had a wife living in London. Deborah did not want to remarry whilst there was a chance that Rogers might still be alive for fear of being charged with bigamy, but in September 1730 she and Franklin entered into a common law marriage. Deborah helped Benjamin considerably during his career. She proved to be an astute business manger and whilst Benjamin ran the printing business, she successfully took charge of the couple's general store. She never accompanied Benjamin overseas, for fear it was said that her plain appearance and simple ways might embarrass her husband in front of his elegant European colleagues. Deborah died of a heart attack in 1784 whilst Benjamin was in England.

Franklin thrived on hard work and his business interests expanded. In 1733 he began to publish *Poor Richard's Almanac* under the guise of a poor man needing money to take care of his carping wife. With the assistance provided by Deborah, Franklin felt able to retire early from his business in 1749, and to turn his attention to science, experiments and inventions. This was the period during which he developed some of his scientific theories and experiments, especially on electricity, that were to dazzle the scientific world. His relative isolation from European science seems to have stimulated his originality. His work was eventually published in England by the Royal Society and in 1752 he conducted his famous kite experiment which Priestley declared was *"the greatest, perhaps, in the whole compass of philosophy since the time of Sir Isaac Newton"*.[10] As the news of his experiments spread Franklin became internationally famous. He received the Royal Society's Copley Medal in 1753 and was elected a Fellow in 1756.

At the same time, he became actively involved in local and state politics. He served his home city of Philadelphia in many ways, such as getting the streets paved and lit, establishing schools, hospitals and a fire department. In 1757 he was sent to London to represent Pennsylvania and other colonies as their Agent in England. He was popular and at ease in London society. His duties did not stop him travelling widely – he visited the philosopher David Hume in Scotland – and pursuing his other interests, especially scientific. Liberal in thought and politics, he had little time for prejudice and superstition, and was drawn naturally to intellectual groups like the Rational Dissenters. He sympathised with their struggle for greater legal recognition and came to admire the character of men like Richard Price and Joseph Priestley. He was an inveterate joiner of clubs and societies and valued particularly his membership of the Club of Honest Whigs which met for supper every other week at the St Paul's Coffee House in London.

The Club had been founded in the early 1760s as a philosophical society, but as the American Revolution proceeded it grew more political and supported the American cause. In effect the Club acted as an intellectual clearing house where liberal views and developments in political affairs, religion and the sciences would be discussed. Franklin enjoyed immensely the cut and thrust of the Club's meetings, its informality and its conviviality. It was at the Club that his friendship with three of its most prominent and distinguished members flourished, the scientist John Canton, Richard Price and Joseph Priestley. Franklin was a generous man and all three were to derive much benefit from their friendship with him.

He and Canton had already collaborated on experiments with electricity, and it was chiefly Franklin who persuaded the Royal Society to award Canton the Copley Medal in recognition of his scientific work. It was inevitable that Franklin would be drawn also to a man of Richard Price's eminence. Price's amiable personality and his mathematical and scientific interests quickly attracted Franklin's attention, and he was very impressed with Price's work on probability and demography (Chapter 3).

Franklin and Priestley
As for Joseph Priestley, his meeting with Franklin marked an important point in his career, transforming him from teacher and preacher to a scientist of international repute. They first met in London late in 1765 when Priestley was still a tutor at the Warrington Academy. Priestley had come to London to see John Canton who, knowing Priestley's growing interest in science, invited Franklin and other distinguished scientists to meet the promising young man.

On the face of it, Franklin and Priestley seemed to have little in common. For a start, the tall, well built Franklin towered over the lean and smaller man. At 60, the worldly Franklin was nearly 30 years older than Priestley, and had

9. John Canton. A physicist and teacher, and friend to Franklin and Priestley

something of a lurid reputation, even, it was said, occasionally attending as a non-member the notorious Hellfire Club. By nature, Franklin had a rather elusive character and liked to keep people guessing, whereas Priestley was characteristically open and forthright. Yet, they were drawn immediately to one another. Priestley was fascinated by the scientific experiments that Franklin and others had performed, and inspired to learn more. Within a few years Priestley had become probably the closest of all Franklin's confidants in England.

When they first met, Priestley already had in mind to write a comprehensive history of electricity and he took the opportunity to ask for Franklin's support for the project and to share with him the proofs of the book he was writing on electricity. Franklin encouraged him throughout and gave him free access to his field-work notes and use of his laboratory equipment. Priestley's *History of Electricity* was rather a hasty and incomplete piece of work but it was well-received and ran to 5 editions during his lifetime.

Even before Priestley's work had been completed, Franklin had become so impressed with his young protégé that he proposed to the Royal Society in 1768 that Priestley should be awarded the Copley Medal. But the proposal was deemed premature. Priestley had to wait until 1772 before receiving the Medal by which time Franklin and his friends had made sure that all the supporting evidence was in place.

Also in 1772 Priestley was elected to the prestigious French Academy of Sciences. Whenever Franklin was visiting France he had lobbied on behalf of his friend to be elected to the Academy. *"I have mentioned him"*, he informed

Richard Price, *"upon every vacancy that has happened since my residence here, and the place has never been bestowed more worthily"*.[11]

The Kite Experiment

It was in June 1752 in Philadelphia that Franklin reportedly performed his most famous experiment which has passed into legend. In a field near the city, accompanied only by his son, he bravely ran a hemp string from a kite to draw down an electric charge from a thundercloud. The current was carried to the ground via the wet twine which was attached to a Leyden jar, a simple device for storing static electricity. His experiment was held as proving conclusively that lightning was actually static electricity. It constituted a significant scientific advance, and before long began to be applied in the construction of lightning rods across Europe and America. In London, St Paul's Cathedral was the first building to have a Franklin lightning rod.

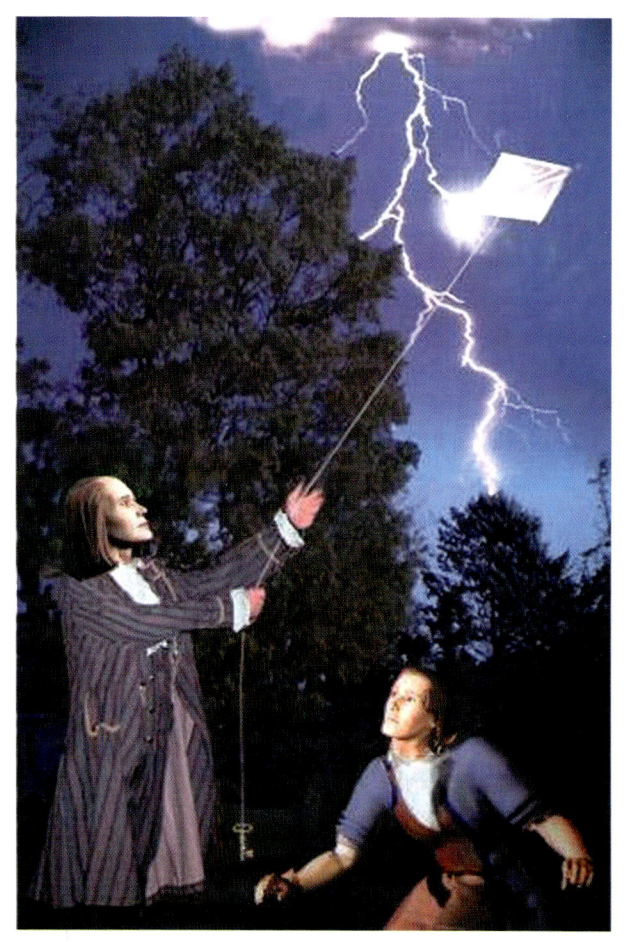

10. A somewhat romantic picture of the kite experiment

In fact the circumstances of the kite experiment are actually all rather mystifying and have been a matter of much debate between historians. Franklin never himself documented in detail the story of his dramatic experiment. Most of what we know about the events of that famous day come from Joseph Priestley's account in his *History of Electricity* published some 15 years later. It seems that Franklin did not publicly say anything about the experiment until October 1752 and then only in a passing reference in the *Pennsylvania Gazette*. He wrote, moreover, in the second person and was careful to say that the experiment had succeeded, not that he had himself performed it. The inference is that his account is more a set of instructions, rather than of actual practice. It is odd too that Franklin, who must have realised the importance of the experiment, should have kept it a secret until October. Consequently, some commentators have even gone as far as suggesting that Franklin, who was well-known to be fond of hoaxes, had in fact invented the whole story.

However, Franklin was always honest about his experiments and the detail recorded in the account given by Priestley was so thorough that it could hardly have been fabricated. It may well be, too, that talking to Priestley about the experiment all those years later he mistook the month it had been carried out and that it was carried out in fact in September rather than June. Certainly, Priestley had no doubts and explained that Franklin's reluctance to document his experiment was due to the ridicule which too commonly attended unsuccessful attempts in science. Such was Priestley's confidence in Franklin that he tried the experiment himself on a stormy day in March 1766 in England. His brother Timothy, who had made the kite, and his wife Mary tried to dissuade him, but he pressed ahead. He did however take the precaution of trailing a chain behind the kite to ground it, and Mary persuaded him not to raise it higher than his head. The outcome is unclear, but there is a tale that a neighbour's curious goose plucked at the chain when lighting struck and was martyred in the cause of science.[12]

The American Revolution
As well as sharing Franklin's scientific interests, Priestley and Richard Price (Chapter 3) were soon openly supporting Franklin in his political efforts on behalf of the American colonists in their disputes with the British government. In 1768 Priestley published his *Essay on Government* and in the following year his *Present State of Liberty in Great Britain and her Colonies*. These two pamphlets set out his own political philosophy, and expressed for the first time his belief in the right of people to rebel against a tyrannical government. In essence, both Priestley and Richard Price saw America as providing the New Society which could set an example to the rest of the world by putting into practice not only national autonomy, but all the other freedoms they held dear, such as freedom of worship, freedom of speech and representative government.

Such views inevitably aroused the hostility of King George III and his government but Priestley and Price persisted in their campaign for the rights of the colonists in the hope that a peaceful settlement could be achieved. Indeed as Priestley notes in his autobiography, Franklin did all in his power to prevent a rupture between the two countries, and dreaded war. But as relations between the two countries deteriorated, Franklin and Priestley became more and more pessimistic at the prospect of an outright war. The more prudent Franklin, conscious of his diplomatic responsibilities, was inclined not to voice his views as openly as his radical friends, but in private he did what he could to encourage them. In 1774 at Franklin's suggestion, Priestley responded by publishing his *Address to Protestant Dissenters of All Denominations* in which he argued that the American colonists had never in fact been subject to the laws of England except voluntarily, and had placed themselves under the British King only out of *"their regard to the country from which they came"*.[13] Such a bold and radical proposition inevitably intensified official displeasure with Priestley. And as war became ever more certain, Franklin's own position in England became untenable and he reluctantly concluded that it was time to make his farewells.

It was with Priestley that Franklin spent his last day in London on 19 March 1775, before leaving for America. They talked about the crisis in America and read the latest American newspapers in the hope of finding something that might serve the American cause by reprinting in the London papers. Priestley recorded that now and again Franklin wept at the news he read.[14] The next day Franklin travelled to Portsmouth for his voyage to America. He left England where he had worked hard for 10 years with a heavy heart. By now he had lost faith in many of his acquaintances there, apart from his closest friends Joseph Priestley and Richard Price, who in his eyes at least stood for all that was honest and virtuous in England.

The New Republic
On his return to America, events turned Franklin's disillusionment with Britain into outright hostility, and he threw himself into working heart and soul for the birth of the new Republic. But the war of independence had first to be won. He was elected to the Second Continental Congress which had been established to organise the war. Washington was appointed as the Commander-in-Chief of the army, and Franklin became the United States first Postmaster General with responsibility for all Post Offices, from Massachusetts to Georgia. He served on other important committees such as negotiating with the Native American Indians and finding supplies of saltpetre. He was also appointed to the committee of five men who drafted in 1776 the Declaration of Independence which formally severed the links with Britain.

Nor did Franklin neglect keeping in touch with his old friends in England. He kept Priestley informed of the progress of the war and in July 1775 told him that, *"Great frugality and great industry are now become fashionable here. Gentlemen who used to entertain with two or three courses, pride themselves now in treating with simple beef and pudding"*.[15]

In December 1776 Franklin was appointed as an ambassador to the Court of Louis XVI in Paris, an important post since France was America's vital ally in its struggle for independence. He sailed for France in October 1777. After a stormy passage he arrived at Nantes so weak that he could hardly stand. He was greeted as a world statesman who had no equal in his wisdom, brilliance and ability. Apparently the ladies of Nantes took one look at his peaked fur cap and rushed back home to dress their hair in the fashion *à la Franklin*. In Paris he was a sensation. He was the darling of the salons and attracted large crowds wherever he went, and, it was said, *"No house was quite in fashion that did not have a Franklin portrait over the chimney piece"*.[16] His time in France indeed proved to be very successful. He secured the active support and goodwill of

11. Franklin enjoys his popularity with the ladies at the Court of Louis XVI

France at a critical time and also enough gold to sustain the impoverished American finances.

The American war may have separated Franklin from his English friends but it was not long before he made new ones in France. His scientific interests naturally drew him to the great chemist Antoine Lavoisier who became a close friend. Madame Lavoisier too admired Franklin and painted his portrait whilst he was in France. Franklin did not however lose touch with Priestley. He wrote in 1782 to Priestley saying how, *"I love you as much as ever, and I love all the honest Souls that meet at the London Coffeehouse. I only wonder how it happen'd that they and my other friends in England, came to be such good Creatures in the midst of so perverse a Generation"*.[17] Franklin also kept Priestley informed of Lavoisier's experiments on combustion. He would, no doubt, have been aware of the scientific dispute that broke out between the two scientists but carefully steered clear of any comment of his own.

Franklin and Priestley continued to correspond freely throughout the War of American Independence and as Norman Beale has pointed out in his excellent book, *Joseph Priestley in Calne*, may well have contributed to the breach which occurred between Priestley and his employer Lord Shelburne in 1780. Since Priestley was well-known to be close to Shelburne and his personal adviser, this left the latter open to accusations by some of his political opponents that he was *"in correspondence with the enemies of his country"*. The accusations were completely false but Shelburne felt the need to fight a duel to clear his name that very nearly cost him his life.

Last Years

In 1785, then in his late seventies, Franklin returned to America. He broke his journey in England where some 60 years earlier the vigorous young Franklin had swum the Thames from Chelsea to the Embankment to entertain onlookers. He was still mentally active but now very tired. He fell asleep for an hour in Southampton's salt water baths, before meeting for the last time a few of his English friends, although there is no record that Priestley was among them.

On his return to America, there was to be no respite for Franklin from public duties. Once he was settled his fellow citizens pressed him to stand for office. He wrote resignedly to a friend, *"they have eaten my flesh and seem resolved to pick my bones"*.[18] He became President of the Executive Council of Pennsylvania, in today's terms State Governor. He served as delegate to the Constitution Convention and signed the new American Constitution to which he made some important contributions. Among his suggestions was that in the Senate every State should have equal representation, but in the House each State should be represented in proportion to its population. One of his last acts was to write an anti-slavery treatise in 1789.

Physically, Franklin was a very big man, weighing over 300 pounds and he had for a long time suffered from gout and bladder stones. In the spring of 1790 a general breakdown of his health forced him to take to his bed. When he left it briefly to have the bed clothes changed, his daughter remarked encouragingly to him that he was going to get better, he characteristically answered, *"I hope not"*.[19]

Benjamin Franklin died on 17 April 1790 at the very advanced age (for the time) of 84. The funeral procession to the old Christ Church burial ground in Philadelphia was the greatest ever seen in the city. Congress voted to wear the customary badge of mourning for one month but otherwise seems to have treated one of its oldest and greatest servants less generously than he deserved. Franklin had persistently asked for some modest office for his grandson, Temple Franklin, who had for several years served him as his secretary, but to no avail. Moreover, Franklin's repeated efforts to get his own accounts settled with the government had never met with any response; consequently when he died he appeared as a debtor. France showed him a warmer appreciation. Mirabeau delivered an impassioned eulogy to the French National Assembly and the Academy of Sciences, and all the revolutionary clubs paid honour to him. A street in Paris near the Trocadero perpetuates his name and the respect and admiration the French have for him.

Conclusion

From very humble beginnings Benjamin Franklin accomplished great things in his life unsurpassed in the eighteenth century in a range of fields. Some might find his moralism spurious and others had little time for his democratic and egalitarian ideas. One of his most impressive characteristics was his capacity for making friends wherever he went. He was simply a marvellously interesting and stimulating person to be with, and his curiosity about everything under the sun made him a most agreeable companion. He made few real enemies and the main contests of his life were confined to political differences. Anna Barbauld (Chapter 3) thought that he was a true hero because he understood common life and all that helped to make it more comfortable.

Joseph Priestley was just one of many distinguished men who fell under Benjamin Franklin's spell and who benefited hugely from his advice, wisdom and generosity. They became the firmest of friends and were genuine collaborators in working for the advance of science and political progress. Even when they were separated Priestley delighted in keeping his former collaborator up to date with his experiments; he wrote from Calne in February 1776 that he was being very successful in his experiments with metals and that Franklin would *"smile when I tell you I do not absolutely despair of the transmutation of metals"* into gold and silver.[20] For his part, Franklin quickly recognised that Priestley was a man of exceptional talent and character. When he called Priestley the "*honest heretic*", this was not meant to be a criticism but simply to express the respect for all the virtues he saw in his friend.

In the creation of the new American nation Franklin's contribution was immense. Priestley too played an important part by bolstering the morale and determination of the American colonists at a critical time in their struggle for independence through his publications and advocacy in Britain on their behalf.

CHAPTER 3

Richard Price
(1723–1791)
Citizen of the World

Richard Price has been described as one of the greatest Welshmen ever. He was a man of many parts. His interests embraced the fields of philosophy, mathematics, finance and the social sciences, all of which benefited from his powerful and original intellectual powers. A Radical Dissenter, his life was devoted to the improvement of knowledge and to the cause of justice and liberty. On his death, Joseph Priestley declared that *"In real candour, I question whether Dr Price ever had a superior"*.[1]

He established an international reputation and his gregarious nature meant that during his lifetime he made friends with many distinguished men in France

12. Richard Price

and America, as well as in Britain, such as Franklin, Jefferson and Condorcet. But none of his friendships surpassed that with Priestley which lasted over 30 years.

The two men had much in common. Both men were products of the eighteenth century Enlightenment and intense idealists. They shared deep interests in political philosophy, science and religion, and in the power of reason and the progress of humankind. Both came from middle-class families with strong Calvinist roots and each came to challenge their Calvinist upbringing. Educated at Dissenting Academies, they later became preachers and teachers at Academies. They strongly supported the American and French Revolutions but neither showed interest in pursuing a political career or creating a political movement. Both were elected to the Fellowship of the Royal Society, and shared a close association with the prominent politician, Lord Shelburne, who later became Prime Minister. When differences between them did arise, the strength of their friendship enabled them to resolve them amicably.

By character, Price was far from the *"cold-hearted rationalist"* as some of his critics have described him. The quality of his character and the goodness of his heart impressed his contemporaries. As Joseph Priestley put it, *"It was not mere mental ability that could enable a man to write like him; it required perfect integrity as well as a sound understanding"*.[2] Time and again one finds him referred to as *"the great and the good Dr Price"*. It was said that at the market near where he lived, when the women selling oranges saw him approaching on his familiar white horse, they cried out *"Make way! Make way for the good Dr Price!"*. A generous man, he readily praised and supported his friends; Priestley was one of many who benefited from his financial assistance. Much concerned with the welfare of all people, he provided help for the prison reformer, John Howard, in his campaign to improve the conditions of those in gaols and hospitals. *"I am ashamed"*, Howard told Price, *"how much I have accumulated your labour; yet I glory in that assistance, to which I owe so much credit in the world"*.[3] Nor did Price's wide-ranging interests mean he neglected his native land or his family, and he returned to South Wales each summer.

Physically, he was small in stature and his health was never robust. He kept himself very active, riding and walking as much as he could, and was convinced of the merit of taking cold baths three or four times a week. Although preaching was his profession, he was not a great orator and his delivery was awkward. It was more to do with his reputation for honesty and the thoughtfulness of his sermons that attracted his large congregations.

Early Days

He was born at Tynton, Glamorgan, in 1723. His father, Rees Price, was a Congregational minister, but at an early age Richard rejected the narrow and strict Calvinist beliefs of his father and became more liberal in his outlook. He was educated privately but after the death of his father in 1739 he went to the Tenter Abbey Academy, a Dissenting college in Moorfields, London. The Academy's main purpose was to prepare men for the ministry, and theological studies naturally took pride of place. However, under a prominent scientist, John Eames, the Academy had established a reputation as the leading Dissenting Academy for scientific education. Eames was a close friend of Isaac Newton, and it is very likely that it was Eames's lectures in applied mathematics that inspired Price's own enthusiasm for the subject. Price, like Priestley, saw no conflict between his vocation for the ministry and his interests in the natural sciences. On the contrary, both firmly believed that demonstrating the order upon which God had founded the Universe would serve to clarify and develop man's understanding of the Deity and his works.

On completion of his studies, Price left the Academy in 1744 to become family chaplain to George Streatfield, a wealthy merchant tailor and Dissenter. Price ministered to various congregations but in 1756 his circumstances were radically changed when his uncle died and left him a house in London on Leadenhall Street. When in the following year Streatfield died leaving Price a financial legacy, he felt secure enough to marry Sarah Blundell, the daughter of a speculator who had been ruined by the South Sea Bubble.

Mrs Price was always frail. By all accounts the marriage was a happy one although Sarah became a chronic invalid and there were no children. Her main enjoyment seems to have been playing cards. Although Price privately considered it a waste of time, he would sit down every evening with her at a card table *"and play until late with a good humour which charmed everybody"*.[4] They moved to a house in Newington Green, then a small but relatively prosperous village near Hackney, where Price became preacher at the Presbyterian chapel.

The move served Price well for it brought him into close contact with a number of important and influential Dissenting families who lived in the area. These were fairly uneventful years compared with those of his later life, but as well as preaching he did have the time to develop his interests in mathematics, theology and moral philosophy. It was at Newington in 1758 that Price published his first important and influential philosophical work, *Review of the Principal Questions of Morals*, in which he formulated his theory of ethics. The essence of his argument was that moral decisions should be made on the basis of individual conscience and reason alone, and not on traditional Christian teaching.

From Obscurity to Limelight
Although Price had a strong sense of public duty he was not particularly ambitious and by nature disliked publicity. He seems to have been quite content to be left alone to enjoy his quiet life at Newington. However, in the early 1760s all that was changed by a turn of events which eventually led among other

things to his international reputation as an expert in insurance, demography and financial reform.

He had become friends with Thomas Bayes, a minister to a Presbyterian chapel in Tunbridge Wells, a man with wide intellectual interests, including mathematics and statistics. Price was some 20 years younger than Bayes, and just how this important friendship came about is not clear. It is possible that Price sought out Bayes on a theological issue, and they shared mutual friends. We know that Price was deeply impressed with Bayes's intellectual gifts, describing him as *"one of the most ingenious men I ever knew"*.[5] When Bayes died in 1761 his relatives asked Price to examine his papers. Among them there were manuscripts devoted to the problems of probability theory.

Price was soon struck by the originality and the potential importance of Bayes's work. He took great pains over a period of two years to check and verify Bayes's calculations, and made additional notes of his own, before submitting them through John Canton to the Royal Society. In 1763 the Society published the work in their Transactions under the title *An Essay towards solving a Problem in the Doctrine of Chances*. Price later submitted further publications on the subject of probability and as a result he was elected to the Fellowship of the Royal Society in 1765.

The essence of the work established a method by which the probability of an event could be estimated from the frequency of its previous occurrences. Not surprisingly, it soon attracted the interest of the commercial and business community, especially the burgeoning insurance services. Reform was badly

13. Thomas Bayes

needed for during the first half of the eighteenth century several over-optimistic insurance schemes had been launched not based on any sound statistical information on life expectancy or mortality rates. Some had quickly collapsed causing considerable public distress and hardship.

In 1771 Price had followed up his work on Bayes's manuscripts with his own publication, *Observations on Reversionary Payments*. Based mainly on mortality statistics drawn from the well-kept parish registers of Northampton, he was able to provide reasonably accurate information on mortality rates for actuarial and other work. The advantages for a properly funded insurance industry were considerable and the publication became the standard work on insurance well into the nineteenth century. It confirmed Price's international reputation as the leading expert on insurance matters. (It is interesting to note too that Bayes's probability theorem underpins a lot of today's advanced statistical work including use in computer search engines.)

Price also used his statistical expertise in other areas of public life. In 1779 he published his *Essay on the Population of England* in which his dire prediction of a falling population stirred up considerable controversy. In the event his calculations were wrong since he was not able to be certain that the birth rate was declining and he ignored the important fact that the death rate was diminishing.[6] The state of the public finances, especially the National Debt, was another important area on which official advice from Price was sought, and the plans he drew up were the subject of lengthy correspondence with the then Prime Minister, William Pitt.

In 1778, the Continental Congress of the United States so highly regarded Price's financial expertise that they had offered him citizenship *"and to receive his assistance in regulating their finances"*.[11] Although Price felt unable to accept the offer, he continued to have considerable influence on political and public affairs in the new country. In 1784 he published *The Importance of the American Revolution and the Means of Making it a Benefit to the World*, which had a remarkable impact in the United States. It contained advice on a great variety of matters from the importance of statistical information for good government, to the best structure of federal government in America. Frustrated in his attempts to promote actual reform in England, he became consoled by the fact that at last his advice in many areas of public life was now not only being listened to, but acted upon. America had in effect become his *"spiritual home"* where it seemed his ideals were at last being realised.[12]

A Friendship Forged
In the mid-1760s Priestley at that time was living in the north of England and it was on one of his regular visits to London in December 1765 that he first met Price. Priestley had come to London with a letter of introduction to John

Canton, a Fellow of the Royal Society, who like Priestley was working on electricity. Canton was well connected, and he soon introduced Priestley to various scientific friends, including Richard Price. They quickly became firm friends. Price's own interest in electricity had arisen through his contact with Benjamin Franklin and he was soon helping Priestley with his experiments on gases and electricity. In the introduction to his book – *History and Present State of Electricity* – Priestley warmly thanked Price "*... for the attention [he] has given to the work, and for the many important services [he has] rendered me with respect to it*". In the summer of 1766 Price was one of several men (Franklin included) who supported Priestley in his successful application to become a Fellow of the Royal Society.

The friendship between Price and Priestley continued to flourish both intellectually and personally. Since both were convivial men, they both particularly enjoyed their membership of the Club of Honest Whigs. Benjamin Franklin and Theophilus Lindsey (Chapters 2 and 6) were also members. When Price and Priestley arrived at the Club arm in arm in the late afternoon, they would have found wine and punch already on the table, and they could look forward to dining later on Welsh rarebit, apple-puffs, porter and beer.

Bowood Group

Price first became associated with Lord Shelburne, the Whig politician, in 1771. Shelburne had enlightened political views and championed religious toleration for the Dissenters. For a short time in 1782–83 he became Prime Minister. The two men quickly formed a friendly working relationship and a mutual affection lasting until Price's death in 1791. Shelburne much respected Price's judgement and frequently sought his advice and help on important political, religious and business questions, and encouraged him to publish his views. He also turned to Price on personal matters; it was Price, aware of how important it was for Priestley to gain some form of patronage for his work, who first suggested to Shelburne that Priestley might be interested in the post of Librarian to Shelburne at his home Bowood House in Calne, Wiltshire, and to act as tutor to his children. After some procrastination, Priestley accepted Shelburne's offer of the appointment in August 1772.

This turned out to be a very important post for the development of Priestley's work as a scientist. Moreover, whilst at Calne he was also able to take full advantage of the company of a number of intellectual and professional men whom Shelburne had gathered together to advise him on a wide range of political, economic and social affairs, the so-called Bowood Group. Price naturally was a member, along with other famous and learned men such as Jeremy Bentham, Benjamin Franklin and Samuel Romilly, the law reformer and Solicitor General.

Religious, Philosophical and Political Differences

As Rational Dissenters, intellectually Price and Priestley held views much in sympathy but it was probably inevitable that with such searching and powerful minds they would at times have their differences.

For a start, in terms of their religious belief, although they both belonged to the Unitarian ministry, in practice they occupied the extreme right and left positions of its theology. Price's belief was basically Arian in that he recognised Christ as created by the Father who sent him as God's messenger and Messiah on earth. As God's creation, Christ was to be worshipped and even looked upon as God. But Price nonetheless denied that Christ was of the same nature or equal in divinity to God. Priestley, on the other hand, moved in his life from Calvinism through Arianism and on to Socinianism. He, like Price, acknowledged God as the one true God, but asserted that Christ was only a man, albeit a virtuous and exceptional man, who was filled with divine inspiration and one who should be revered as such.

They also approached philosophical problems in quite different ways. Whilst Price was a mathematician and an intellectual at home with abstract ideas, Priestley was an experimental scientist who relied more on practice and observation, rather than theory. Their religious and philosophical differences were brought into the open in 1777 when Priestley published his *Disquisitions relating to Matter and Spirit* in which he clearly and boldly set out his views on the soul. Price's two main disagreements with Priestley centred around the latter's discussion of 'materialism' and free will.

As regards materialism, Priestley believed that God had created the world of mere matter, and that included mind and soul, all of which was infused with God's divine spirit. He argued that man's mind and soul dwelt as one in the body and were actually part of man's material being, and therefore at death both died and putrefied. Only by a direct exertion of God in the future general Resurrection would there be a miraculous rebirth. Price, on the other hand, was one step nearer to the Christian position and believed strongly in the opposite view. He believed in the immortality of man and that the soul was an immaterial substance, capable of thought and perceptions, and that at death it slept whilst awaiting resurrection for eternal life. Many others, besides Price, were deeply offended by Priestley's view on the immortality and immateriality of the soul, and Dr Johnson was heard to utter, *"Ah Priestley, an evil man, Sir. His work unsettled everything"*.[7]

The two men also differed sharply over the notions of free will and determinism, issues which were debated widely during the eighteenth century. In an Appendix to his *Disquisitions*, Priestley published his *Doctrine of Philosophic Necessity Illustrated* in which he maintained that humans had no free will in so far that *"all things, past, present and to come, are precisely what the Author of nature really intended them to be, and has made provision for"*. He therefore argued in favour of the existence of a benign form of determinism in which, like the rest of nature, man's mind is subject to the laws of causation. Since a benevolent God had created those laws, Priestley contended that eventually the world would be perfected.

Price, on the other hand was a moral libertarian who believed that there was an eternal moral law which was constant, in the same way as there was a mathematical law. In his system the freedom of will was essential to religion and morality. People in other words were left free by God to determine what they believe to be their duty, right or wrong, by the exercise of their own reason. Thus, in the last analysis men and women were the arbiters of their own fate and there was no room for any form of predestination.

Although both Price and Priestley stuck resolutely to their respective opinions, the debate between them had none of the personal animosity which often characterised important eighteenth century controversies, notably that between Priestley and Bishop Horsley (Chapter 8). The Price/Priestley exchanges were conducted intelligently and in a good tempered manner. They gave rise to no lasting enmity; indeed it encouraged them to publish their differences jointly in 1778 in a work entitled *A Free Discussion of the Doctrines of Materialism and Philosophical Necessity*. The book allowed both men to explain in considerable detail their respective positions over the problems on which they disagreed; it is generally felt however to have added little new to the arguments of previous writers. It rather tells us more about the mutual respect and quality of their friendship.

There were differences, too, between the two men in terms of political philosophy. Until the last 20 or so years of his life, Price had paid little attention to political issues but given his strong liberal beliefs found himself drawn inexorably into the revolutions that occurred in America and France towards the end of the eighteenth century. His political pamphleteering, first in support of the American and then the French Revolution, propelled him into the front line of political debate and controversy. Within the space of a few years his political involvement made him one of the most controversial men in Great Britain, which, unfairly perhaps, has in historical terms overshadowed his achievements elsewhere.

Price believed that the American Revolution was one of the most important events in the history of mankind. He had publicly committed himself to the support of the American colonists in their struggle for independence in his pamphlet, published in 1776, and entitled *Observations on the Nature of Civil Liberty and Policy of the War with America*. This set out the rights of the colonists, the justice of their cause and the problems it would cause for Britain. Inevitably it attracted criticism of Price from the government and prominent people, including John Wesley, and, ominously for the future, Edmund Burke (Chapter 10). It was welcomed enthusiastically however by many people, and within a few months over 60,000 copies had been sold. The Duke of Cumberland told Price that he had read the pamphlet until he was nearly blind, which prompted his fellow peer Lord Ashburton to comment that it was remarkable that the Duke had been blinded by a book that had opened the eyes of the kingdom.[8] Price's *Observations* and his other publications in support of the American Revolution were highly regarded by Americans since they helped to convince them of the justice of their cause. Support, too, for Price was to come from an unexpected quarter when the City of London, which had been strongly opposed to the war in America, presented him with the Freedom of the City for his campaign.

Priestley greeted Price's *Observations* as an *"excellent pamphlet"* for which he *"sat up till after one o'clock to read"*.[9] Nonetheless, it does illustrate some of the differences in their respective political philosophy. Priestley certainly shared his friend's objectives when issues of freedom, justice and liberty were concerned, but he approached them in a more pragmatic way. For Price, the issues of freedom and self government were philosophical, not to do with legality or with historical or contemporary politics, but with morality. This political position was consistent with the importance he attached to freedom of choice and individual responsibility in his moral philosophy. He believed that the rights of the American rebels in their struggle for political freedom had to be defended because they were rights that belonged to mankind as a whole.

Priestley, on the other hand, reasoned not from general principles, but from a much more practical and utilitarian approach. In his work on the *First Principles of Government* he states clearly that *"we are so little capable of arguing a priori in matters of government that it should seem experiments only can determine how far this power of legislature ought to extend"*.[10] In contrast to Price's conviction that individuals had natural rights preceding society, Priestley argued that all people lived in society for their mutual advantage and reasoned that in fact their happiness is the great standard by which every thing relating to the state must finally be determined. Thus by propounding the happiness of the majority as the main criterion for making political judgements, Priestley clearly anticipated the *Greatest Happiness Principle*, which later formed the basis of Jeremy Bentham's political philosophy.

The French Revolution
The success of the American Revolution encouraged Price to believe that it would inspire other nations to curb the use of absolute power and to grant more freedom to their peoples. He therefore took a keen interest in many other struggles overseas. Close to home, he supported the political movements pressing for more Irish independence and the reform of the Irish Parliament. He was very disappointed when a revolt by political reformers in the United Provinces (now the Netherlands) was crushed. But it was the events in France that

captured most of his attention and were to lead to the most controversial and difficult period of his life.

In a letter to Thomas Jefferson then in Paris, Price greeted the fall of the Bastille in July 1789 as marking *"a Revolution that must astonish Europe; that shakes the foundation of despotic power; and that probably will be the commencement of a general reformation in the governments of the world which have hitherto been little better than usurpations on the rights of mankind"*.[13] Then later in November 1789, on the anniversary of Britain's Glorious Revolution of 1688, Price preached his famous sermon entitled *A Discourse on the Love of our Country*. The *Discourse*, which was published, is not a particularly radical or inflammatory tract and most of his comments were sensible and reasonably balanced. Price set out thoughtfully the main political problems facing any civilised nation of that time and advocated a universal form of citizenship. He endorsed Priestley's views that the chief blessings of mankind are *"Truth, Virtue and Liberty"*. Only towards the end did he refer specifically to the French Revolution but unfortunately in words which caused such alarm among conservatives and none more so than with Edmund Burke. In a bout of enthusiastic rhetoric, Price welcomed the Revolution as the *"ardour of liberty catching and spreading; a general amendment beginning in human affairs; the dominion of kings changed for the dominion of laws, and the dominion of priests giving way to the dominion of reason and conscience"*. He called for oppressors of the world to *"Tremble"*, and to *"restore to mankind their rights: and consent to the correction of abuses, before they and you are destroyed together"*.[14]

Conflict with Edmund Burke

Price had gone too far. His remarks convinced the establishment and the other opponents of the Dissenters that he, like Priestley, was another dangerous revolutionary, and set off a chain reaction of events in England.

Matters became worse when Price, injudiciously, at a celebratory dinner of the Revolution Society proposed a toast in July 1790 to *"The Parliament of Britain, may it become a National Assembly"*. Price tried to calm down the resulting criticism by pointing out that his intention, far from being revolutionary, was merely to advocate that the British Parliament should become more representative. But the damage had been done. In November 1790 the formidable Edmund Burke, ironically at one time a friend of both Price and Priestley, published his famous work *Reflections on the Revolution in France*.

Regarded by many as one of the finest works on politics in the English language, the *Reflections* is now chiefly remembered for Burke's momentous prophecy that only bloodshed and anarchy would follow the French Revolution. Burke also made clever use of the book to mount a powerful attack on Price and his associates (Chapter 10).

Burke was a stout supporter of the Established Church, the monarchy and aristocracy. He instinctively distrusted Price's zeal for reform and suspected that the Dissenters were at bottom a subversive force within the State and that their agitation for full freedom of worship was merely a beginning to a full attack on the Church establishment, monarchy and the constitution. Burke, in a scathing attack on Price and his fellow intellectuals, dismissed them as nothing more than misguided and abstract intellectuals, *"the hopping insects of the hour"*, who lacked practical experience and simply offered solutions based on theory and general principles. Price was portrayed as a mere propagandist who, like other revolutionaries, were *"unacquainted with the world in which they are so fond of meddling"*, and too ready to assert the violation of rights with too little regard to the consequences.[15]

Price was profoundly upset by the vehemence of Burke's personal attack on him and on his arguments. His health was failing and he declined to get involved in any controversy. Privately, Price wrote to Priestley condemning Burke's criticisms as *"abuse"* but his only public response was a brief note in the fourth edition of his *Discourse on the Love of our Country*.

It fell to Joseph Priestley, and the radical pamphleteer Thomas Paine, to lead the most powerful counter-attack to Burke. In 1791 Priestley rushed to the defence of his friend by publishing his pamphlet *Letters to the Right Honourable Edmund Burke*. With clear and ruthless logic, he pointed out the weaknesses in

14. A Gillray cartoon of 1790 in which Price incurs the wrath of both Church and King.

15. Edmund Burke runs the gauntlet of some contemporary political and literary figures, including Richard Price and Anna Barbauld (second and third from the left), for his attack on the French Revolution

Burke's polemic, and particularly deplored the way in which Burke had used ridicule to belittle Price. Priestley used his pamphlet to present his own aspirations for peace and goodwill among nations. Thomas Paine was likewise deeply disappointed and shocked by Burke's intemperate attack. His response was to publish in 1791 the first part of his great and enduring work *The Rights of Man*. Similarly, Mary Wollstonecraft, the famous feminist who greatly admired Price and shared many of his aspirations, rallied to the support of her friend and wrote in his defence her political pamphlet, *Vindication of the Rights of Man*.

His opponents however continued to attack Price right up to his death and beyond. The conservative political journal *The Anti-Jacobin* did not begin publishing until some six years after Price's death, but became the main vehicle for perpetuating the cruel attacks on him, damning him as the *Arch Devil* and the *Revolution Sinner*. The following verse is typical of criticisms made of him:

> *Let our vot'ries then follow the glorious advice,*
> *In the Gunpowder Legacy left us by Price,*
> *Inflammable matter to place grain by grain*
> *And blow up the State with the torch of Tom Paine.*[16]

Final Years

With his health deteriorating fast, Price decided to resign from his Hackney pulpit and preached his valedictory service there on 20 February 1791. A few days later he developed a high fever which aggravated a bladder complaint. He lingered for a while but in the early hours of 19 April he died, "*praising God for his goodness*".[17] Although he had left instructions that he did not want a public funeral, his friends insisted upon organising one. Most of Price's Dissenting friends were there along with many other prominent people. Six Dissenting ministers, among them Joseph Priestley, carried him to his grave in London's Bunhill Fields.

On 1 May 1791, Priestley delivered the funeral oration at Hackney which took the form of a heart-felt personal tribute to his friend. He mentioned that Price and he had disagreed on many things but both drew comfort from the belief that *"virtuous men shall meet after death in a state of happiness"*.[18] Priestley was to cherish the memory of his friend until the end of his own life. In his exile in America, a portrait of Richard Price was hung along with others in the study of his home in Pennsylvania. Such portraits, he remarked to another great friend, Lindsey, *"Though dead, they seem to speak, and tend to inspire good sentiments"*.

Conclusion
On the surface Richard Price lived a mostly placid and uneventful life. Introverted, gentle and scholarly by nature, he was not a man of action, and fame attracted him little. He was utterly without jealousy or malice towards others. He was more disappointed than angered by Burke's fierce attack on him which probably hastened the end of his life. The range of his intellectual interests and the forthrightness and courage he showed in advancing his opinions were truly remarkable. The books and pamphlets he wrote during his lifetime made important contributions to the fields of political and moral philosophy, theology, parliamentary reform, science and financial affairs.

It is true that many of his hopes and his influence, at least as far as Britain was concerned, died with him. In terms of his religious beliefs, his Arianism gave ground to the more extreme form of Unitarianism espoused by Priestley. His moral and political idealism both underrated the difficulties and inherent dangers of attempting large scale reform, and the extent to which men were prepared to listen and were moved by moral considerations.

Perhaps it is significant that Richard Price has enjoyed a higher esteem in America where he has achieved a more enduring legacy. The intellectual and courageous support he gave to the cause of independence had a significant impact on its eventual success. The new country greatly respected his abilities and readily used his advice in tackling the problems it faced on independence. And Price's consideration of Unitarianism in *"its broadest possible terms"* had considerable influence on the development of American Unitarianism.[19]

Richard Price and Joseph Priestley were the closest of friends; they encouraged and supported each other in numerous ways. They both stirred up more than their fair share of controversy. The difference was that whereas Priestley enjoyed crossing swords with others, it was something Price would shun if he could. What is clear however is that some of the ideas on which they collaborated, such as the relationship between Church and State, the moral problems of political corruption and the right to liberty of conscience in religious matters, have a decidedly modern reference. That they were prepared to subject one another's philosophical and political ideas to the most critical and searching examination without any rancour is testament to the strength of their friendship, and to the honesty and candour which governed their lives.

CHAPTER 4

John Wilkinson
(1728–1808)
The Great Iron Maker

'Iron-Mad' Wilkinson was a most remarkable man. A great iron master, he played a dominant role in the early Industrial Revolution of Great Britain. In the course of his life, as an inventor and entrepreneur, he built an enormous industrial empire embracing ironworks, canals, mines, farming and banking. A forceful and passionate personality, and renowned for his eccentricities, he was both widely respected and feared. He became the brother-in-law of Joseph Priestley and their friendship thrived. It proved to be a very significant relationship for both men. Wilkinson benefited from Priestley's scientific advice and researches, and at various crucial stages of his life Priestley and his family received substantial financial and other assistance from the iron master.

Character
John Wilkinson's achievements show he had some exceptional qualities. First and foremost, he was a far-sighted entrepreneur who could combine technological leadership with enormous drive and business acumen. Always ready to seek out new ways of doing things, he was prepared to take expensive risks but not without careful thought and planning. He was also a great organiser, a tireless and determined man who managed his various enterprises with notable efficiency. A good judge of character, he always took considerable care to select able people to help run undertakings. He could, moreover, be a very generous man, as we shall see from his help for the Priestley family, and most unusually for the time, he provided pensions for his former employees. Like Priestley, he was born into a non-conforrmist family. He seems to have adopted Unitarian views, but he kept his religion to himself; and was at various times described as Anglican, Methodist and free thinker as well.[1] Stoical by nature he took life's ups and downs in his stride. In public affairs, he was liberal in his views, supported the French and American Revolutions and lived by his maxim that *"manufacture and commerce will always flourish most where Church and King interfere least"*.[2]

There was nonetheless a darker side to his character. He was determined to have his own way and admitted to James Watt that he could not be *"angry by halves*". He certainly could be very ruthless when necessary, and had the reputation for some less-than-honest business dealings. In the course of his life he made many enemies. Lord Dundonald – a neighbour and business rival – castigated him as *"one of the most hard-hearted, malevolent old scoundrels now existing in Britain"*.[3] His family life was acrimonious. He became estranged from his father and in the later part of his life his relations with his brother William became very bitter indeed. He was a philanderer and had a number of mistresses. During his marriage with his second wife, Mary, he formed a relationship with Ann Lewis, one of his housekeepers, by whom in his seventies he had three illegitimate children.

Early Life

John Wilkinson was born in Clifton, Cumberland in 1728. His father, Isaac Wilkinson, was a farmer who worked occasionally at a nearby iron smelting furnace. When John was 12 years old the family moved to Backbarrow, a small industrial centre near Lake Windermere and he helped to run an iron furnace there. The venture was successful enough for Isaac to send John to the

16. John Wilkinson

Dissenting Academy in Kendal. A younger son, William, completed his education at the school established by Joseph Priestley at Nantwich, Cheshire, and it was there that Priestley met Mary Wilkinson, John's sister, whom Priestley married in 1762.

The Priestleys' marriage was a most happy and successful one. However, we know that Priestley seems to have expected more financially from the marriage; he rather churlishly remarked on the fact that his wife had a meagre dowry because Isaac Wilkinson had become impoverished in his old age.

Isaac was ambitious, and once his son John had completed his apprenticeship in Liverpool as a merchant ironmonger, he decided that the time had come to expand by running a furnace of his own. In 1753, the family purchased the Bersham Ironworks in North Wales. Previously the Ironworks had been worked with charcoal with poor results, but the iron maker, Abraham Darby, had perfected at his Coalbrookdale works the use of coke rather than charcoal for smelting iron, and this now made the Bersham furnace appear to be a good investment. It was at Bersham that John married his first wife Ann Mawdsley in 1755, a wealthy heiress, who much to his distress, died aged only 22 shortly after the birth of a daughter, Mary.

Despite expanding its range of engineering components and armaments, the Bersham furnace did not prove to be as successful as was hoped. In 1761 Isaac Wilkinson retired to Bristol, and the ironworks were taken over by John and his brother William who between them quickly turned its fortunes around.

Industrial Empire

By 1774 John Wilkinson had patented a new type of cannon-borer for boring iron to great precision and Bersham became renowned for its production of guns and other armanents. Consequently, the works greatly prospered, and are said to have manufactured cannons for both sides in the American War of Independence.

The invention of the cannon-borer was also vitally important for the development of machine tools and played a major part in the final perfection of the steam engine. James Watt, the famous Scots engineer, had been frustrated in his attempts to obtain cast iron cylinders that were machined precisely enough for a working piston to contain steam pressure when in regular motion. On the recommendation of Matthew Boulton, a friend of Wilkinson, he approached the iron master who successfully produced a cylinder in 1775 which met Watt's requirements perfectly. Within weeks of receiving the new cylinder, Watt got his first steam engine to work. Delighted with the engine's much improved performance, Boulton and Watt insisted that all the parts for their steam engines should in future be made by John Wilkinson.

The success at the Bersham works inspired John to look for further opportunities for expansion. He had become increasingly interested in developing

17. One of the few extant buildings associated with the Bersham Ironworks. It was built in 1775 probably as a cannon foundry

the mineral and coal rich countryside to the south of Wolverhampton, and in building a furnace there, especially in the Bradley district of Bilston. Although he was becoming a relatively wealthy man, he still lacked sufficient capital for the necessary investment; it was only after his second marriage in 1763 to Mary Lee, aged 40 and very wealthy, that he was able to acquire the land he needed at Bradley. The furnace he erected there, known as the *Mother Furnace*, is generally recognised as marking the beginning of the Industrial Revolution in South Staffordshire, and key to the development of his mightiest ironworks.

Ever restless and ambitious, John Wilkinson sought to expand his business interests wherever he could during the remainder of his life. He steadily acquired numerous estates and properties throughout England and Wales. The range of his business ventures was breathtaking. As well as several ironworks he built up interests in mines, smelters, canals, banks and agriculture. In 1772 he was one of the chief subscribers to the Iron Bridge project over the River Severn, insisting that it should be made of iron. In 1787 he successfully manufactured the world's first iron boat which was put to use as a canal barge. He collaborated with Boulton and Watt in the development of the Cornish copper mines. Perhaps his most gigantic task was to cast and make 40 miles of iron pipes and pumping engines for the Paris Waterworks. This huge contract had to overcome enormous problems. Wilkinson had much trouble with pirates who threatened his ships, the Royal Navy press ganged his sailors, and the Government wrangled with him over export licences.

In 1792 Wilkinson bought the Brymbo Hall estate in Denbighshire where he installed furnaces which, along with his other works, enabled him to capitalise on the war with France that broke out in 1793. It is estimated that by 1796 he

18. Bridge over the River Severn at Coalbrookdale built by the iron founders Wilkinson and Darby between 1777–79. It was the world's first cast iron bridge successfully erected

was producing about one-eighth of the nation's entire iron output (15,274 tons). His iron-madness reached its peak; he became obsessed with making almost everything around him of iron. He had an iron desk and an iron bed. He even made iron shoes but found them unworkable. He collected iron coffins and built a massive iron obelisk to mark his grave.

Priestley and Wilkinson
On the face of it, one might not have suspected that the two men would get on so well. Priestley's intellectual interests, his propensity to debate differences and his preaching would hardly appeal to the straight talking, none-too-scrupulous and hard-headed businessman whose religious beliefs were hard to fathom. Since both liked their own way, they could be difficult and stubborn men. Nevertheless, their dealings with one another were pleasant enough. And the feelings expressed in the considerable amount of correspondence which passed between them over many years – 64 letters in all – show a high degree of warmth and mutual respect.[4] Importantly too for the relationship, John Wilkinson also had a deep affection for his sister Mary, Priestley's wife. It was Mary who played a key role in ensuring that the friendship between her brother and husband prospered. She made sure that Wilkinson was always a welcome member of the Priestley family, a gesture which he deeply appreciated.

Although Wilkinson prided himself on being more of a practical man than a theoretical inventor, he nonetheless had a creative side which was stimulated by his association with Priestley. The latter made frequent visits to Wilkinson's Grange-over-Sands estate and kept Wilkinson closely informed of the results of his important work on gases and metals in the hope that they might help Wilkinson's experiments in smelting and metallurgy. Both men had a particular interest in the differing properties between cast iron, malleable iron, annealed iron and steel. Although Wilkinson claimed that he *"could never understand the fellow"*, he much appreciated being able to learn from Priestley's research and the light it threw on the chemistry of manufacturing processes. When living in Birmingham, Priestley, as a member of the Lunar Society, was able to help Wilkinson meet and exchange ideas with other Society members, notably Watt and Boulton. These personal links proved very influential in the transmission of theory to practical application in the early stages of the Industrial Revolution.

Priestley's own scientific work benefited too from the relationship. When he was preparing for and conducting his experiments, Wilkinson took care that the scientist was well provided with equipment and suitable vessels to contain the various liquids and gases he produced.

Financial Assistance to Priestley

The considerable financial generosity shown by Wilkinson to Priestley and other members of his family was a highly important aspect of the friendship between the two men.

Priestley was often hard up. Throughout his life he was frequently helped by his many friends to buy books and to finance his experiments. When he left the employment of his patron Lord Shelburne in 1780, he admitted that his affairs *"wore rather a cloudy aspect"*.[5] Although he continued to receive a pension of £150 a year from Shelburne he badly needed to find a new home and employment to support his growing family. By this time John Wilkinson had become a very wealthy man (he was estimated to be worth around £80,000 which was a very large sum in those days) and he proposed that the Priestley family should settle near him in the Black Country. When Priestley secured employment as a minister of the New Meeting Chapel in Birmingham, John Wilkinson, with help from his brother William, lost no time in finding a large and suitable house for the Priestley family at Fairhill on the outskirts of the city.

From then onwards John was a frequent visitor to the Priestley's family home, and showed a deep concern for the welfare of their daughter and three sons. After his only child, Mary, had died in 1786 he decided to adopt Joseph's eldest son, Joseph Priestley jr, and indeed envisaged him as a potential heir to his business. That said, Wilkinson was not one to let sentimentality get in the way of business, and after four years apprenticeship the younger Priestley's progress proved to be unsatisfactory and he was dismissed, much to his father's disappointment. Wilkinson also refused to employ another son of Priestley's, William, who was temperamental and not easily disciplined.

Increasingly, Priestley and his family became dependent on the success of his brother-in-law and the financial assistance which he was providing for them. On several occasions Priestley openly acknowledged his generosity. Wilkinson, for example, played a notably important part in helping Priestley to construct and equip the first class, but very costly, laboratory which he required for his experiments at his new home in Birmingham. Priestley's children also benefited from Wilkinson's generosity. In the early 1790s when they first settled in America, Wilkinson gave them property there together with a large number of shares in the French East India Company.

But it was Priestley himself who remained the main beneficiary. In 1791 the iron master helped Priestley to repay a loan of £600 which the latter had incurred writing his important pamphlet in reply to Burke's *Reflections on the Revolution in France* (Chapter 10). At that time Priestley also badly needed money to help his son Joseph to set up a business in Manchester, which unfortunately proved unsuccessful. When later that year the Birmingham riots destroyed Priestley's home and his precious laboratory, it was to Wilkinson he turned for help. The iron master provided him with £500 and a house for the family at Clapton in East London. In a further act of generosity, he gave £5,000 to Benjamin Franklin to invest in France on Priestley's behalf so that money would be available if any of the Priestley family decided to move to that country.

Around the same time, Priestley had begun to make some unwise investments in French Government bonds and he persuaded his brother-in-law to do likewise. Wilkinson invested £5,000 in the French funds in his own name but stipulated the interest should be paid to Priestley. Remarkably, Wilkinson soon made a further investment of another £5,000 worth of French bonds and promised to transfer the whole investment of £10,000 to Priestley.[6] The investment was expected to produce an income of £600 a year for Priestley. However, it seems a formal act of transfer never took place. Given the growing turmoil in France, it is not surprising that all these the investments were quickly seen to be poor decisions, and may well have hastened Priestley's decision to emigrate to America in the winter of 1793–94.

Later in 1796, the £10,000 in the French funds was sequestrated by the French Government, and Priestley wrote to Wilkinson deploring the fact that if the money had been held in America it could have yielded more than £20,000. Wilkinson again responded positively; he agreed that his brother-in-law could effectively draw a pension of £200 annually on the iron master's bank *"till the money in the French funds came to be productive"*.[6] Although this arrangement lasted until 1804, it is not clear how much use Priestley in fact made of it. Overall however, it seems clear that these foreign exchange speculations were ill-judged and proved most unfortunate for both men.

Yet another example of Wilkinson's generosity occurred in 1796/97. An expensive and bitter dispute with his brother William had seriously weakened

John's own financial position and he was forced to issue instructions that all debts to him were to be called in. It was reckoned that by this time Priestley owed his brother-in-law the very large sum of $59,000 or the equivalent then of roughly £15,000. No wonder Priestley was horrified by the demand and feared that he might well be forced into bankruptcy. He wrote to Wilkinson admitting that by relying on the latter's generosity, he had misunderstood his intentions and thought the money was more in the nature of a gift rather than a loan. Fortunately, and much to Priestley's relief, John Wilkinson decided to withdraw his demand.

But Priestley's finances remained precarious. His lectures in America were not well attended and his new house was costing much more to build than the earlier estimate. He was much concerned for the future of his daughter, Sally, when her husband's business failed. He thought he could help his daughter, and at least make some repayments to his brother-in-law, if he made one final visit to France in 1797 in an attempt to get access to the £10,000 that Wilkinson had deposited there for him. However, he was not in good health and was dissuaded by his son Joseph from doing so and nothing came of this initiative.

Funeral

During the last five years of his life, John Wilkinson suffered from ill health. He died at his works in Bradley in 1808 at the age of 80, probably from complications of diabetes or gout. The preparations he made for this death, including the funeral arrangements, reflected the eccentric character of the man. He had prepared carefully for his death and always kept a heavy cast iron coffin at each of his residences in case it was needed. Wilkinson had a particularly macabre sense of humour and a favourite joke of his was to lie in a coffin and then seemingly rise from the dead once his guests were ushered in. He also liked offering the coffins to his guests as gifts but apparently had no takers.[7]

Wilkinson left specific instructions that he was to be buried as simply as possible at his home at Castlehead on the edge of Morecambe Bay but in the event the funeral turned into a tragicomedy. For a start, his executors rejected the use of an iron coffin and chose one made of lead and wood. When the driver of the hearse opted for a short cut across the Bay, the weight of the coffin and the sudden incoming tide forced the funeral party to run for their lives leaving the coffin in the surf. After it was retrieved, the coffin finally arrived at Castlehead. Four attempts were made to bury it. First, it was found that the lead coffin was too large for the master iron coffin into which it was to be placed. A larger iron coffin was immediately ordered from the Bradley works but meanwhile the body was temporarily buried in the garden. It was placed in the new coffin when it arrived but then a new difficulty arose due to the fact that the soil of a permanent site proved too shallow. Whilst a hole in the rock was being blasted, poor Wilkinson was taken back into the garden and re-interred

19. John Wilkinson Memorial at Lindale, Cumbria

once more. Even then he enjoyed no peace. In 1828 his coffin was removed to the nearby village of Lindale. There, the King of the Iron masters now lies in an unmarked grave in the churchyard, but a memorial to him has been erected in the village.

Sadly too, the vast industrial empire built by Wilkinson during his lifetime soon went into a quick decline. The depression that followed the Napoleonic Wars generally harmed the iron industry, but more significantly it was a very costly and protracted legal dispute between the trustees appointed by Wilkinson and his nephew, Thomas Jones, that brought down the finances of the huge estate. Within 20 years the Bersham works were derelict and the remains of the Wilkinson empire were sold off.

The great iron master attracted his fair share of myths and legends. His fame and popularity among working people led to the belief that be would revisit one of his major works, that at Bradley, on the seventh annual anniversary of his death. On that day, thousands of people assembled at Monmore Green near Bilston expecting him to appear on his familiar grey horse as he rode to see what had happened to his works during the past seven years.[8]

Conclusion

Of all the important friendships Joseph Priestley made during his lifetime, the one with John Wilkinson stands out as the most unusual. They shared of course a strong interest in scientific discovery and its application to industry. But their characters were very different. Of the two Wilkinson comes across as shrewder and harder headed, and he was more in touch with the working man. He might sympathise with Priestley's political and religious views, but he knew when it was wise to keep a low profile. He was astute enough to counsel Priestley against using the reference to "*gunpowder*" in that ill-fated sermon Priestley delivered on Guy Fawkes Day in 1785 (Chapters 1 and 10). Wilkinson too, whilst a man of great drive, took his time in reaching decisions, in contrast to the impetuous Priestley who rushed quickly from one task to the next.

In practical terms, both men benefited much from their friendship. Wilkinson was able to take advantage of his brother-in-law's scientific discoveries and expertise, and Priestley and his family came to depend heavily on the iron master's generosity.

Although never admitting it, Wilkinson did in some ways suffer from his close association with Priestley. After the Birmingham riots of 1791 which destroyed several Dissenters' homes, besides Priestley's, Wilkinson feared for the safety of his own property. He adopted what amounted to a siege mentality to the outside world and mounted guns and armed forces around his works to protect them. Moreover, he developed a some what paranoid hatred of Birmingham because of the suffering some of its inhabitants had inflicted on his brother-in-law and family. Consequently, he lost some of his former enthusiasm for the work he had been doing with the great Midland engineers, such as Boulton and Watt, and this affected his business dealings with them.

CHAPTER 5

Anna Barbauld
(1743–1825)
Writer and Poet at the Dawn of Romanticism

In his memoirs Joseph Priestley referred to his friend, Anna Barbauld, as *"one of the best poets that England can boast of"*.[1] As we shall see, however, her relationship with him, although close, was by no means straightforward.

Walpole, Goldsmith, Coleridge and Wordsworth all thought highly of Anna Barbauld, and Queen Charlotte, the wife of George III, declared that *"if she is an enthusiast in anything it is an admiration of Mrs Barbauld"*.[2] As a writer and poet, she took advantage of the literary opportunities which had opened up for women in the eighteenth century, and she is now recognised as having had an important influence on the emergence of the British Romantic Movement. Her pamphlets and books also provide an acute insight into the social, cultural and political scene of the age in which she lived. The variety of her writing styles,

20. Anna Barbauld

and the subjects she covered during her lengthy career, are very impressive. Her poetry expressed a range of emotions from the light-heartedness and humour of the *Washing Day* and the *Inventory of Dr Priestley's Study*, to her sombre reflections in poems such as *On the King's Illness* and *Eighteen Hundred and Eleven*.

She was in her element in the age of pamphlets. Although Anna did not share the radical feminist views of some of her contemporaries such as her friend Mary Wollstonecraft, she sympathised with many of their opinions on education, marriage and women's rights and was prepared to write forthrightly about them. Often referred to as the *"sensible Mrs Barbauld"*, her ideas were always expressed clearly and perceptively, and during her lifetime her talent had a wide popular appeal.

Yet, by the middle of the nineteenth century she had fallen out of favour. In the more conservative times that followed the French Revolution, many of the romantic poets whom she had inspired turned against her. During the nineteenth century, most of the critical comment on her work was confined mainly to her hymns and children's verse, and she was inclined to be dismissed as a writer who was little more than a moralist or *"national nanny"*. Only relatively recently with the rise of feminist literary criticism has her rightful reputation and importance been re-appraised and restored.

Early Years

Anna Laetitia Barbauld was born in 1743 at Kibworth in Leicestershire. She was the eldest child of a schoolmaster and his wife, the Rev. John and Mrs Jane Jennings Aikin. Both parents were Presbyterian Dissenters. Anna received a conventional domestic education from her mother but soon persuaded her father to let her learn Latin and Greek and to have free use of his extensive library. Even so her personal and educational development might well have proved narrow and restrictive but for the move of the family to Warrington in 1758. Her father had been invited to take up an appointment at the newly founded Dissenting Academy at Warrington. As well as Priestley, the Academy had attracted as tutors an exceptional group of men and women. Their liberal ideas and distinction in literature, science and theology gave Warrington a reputation of being the *"Athens of the North"*. It was in this stimulating environment that Anna, a spirited and lively girl of 15, now found herself. The next 15 years which she spent there were very influential and probably to become the happiest period of her life.

By all accounts Anna possessed great beauty. She was small and elegant, with a fine complexion and brilliant blue eyes. She quickly attracted several suitors. Indeed, we know that a wealthy farmer followed Anna from Kibworth to Warrington to seek her father's consent to marry her. Anna escaped his unwelcome importunities by jumping over a garden wall. The disconsolate farmer went home to spend the rest of his life as a bachelor although he took care that the one book he possessed, the *Works of Mrs Barbauld*, splendidly bound, adorned his parlour to the end of his days.[3]

The intellectual and cultural atmosphere of the Warrington Academy provided the perfect setting for Anna's first serious poetry. She received encouragement from two principal sources, her brother John Aikin, and from Joseph and Mary Priestley. The Priestleys arrived at the Academy in 1761 when Anna was 18 and, as her first real friends outside her family, they were to have a profound effect on Anna's intellectual and personal development. Joseph, very much the educationalist, recognised her talents and soon set about broadening her horizons. But it was Mary, who was the same age and shared her interests, who became her closest and most treasured friend. When the Priestleys left the Academy in 1767 for Leeds, Anna wrote to Mary her first known poem entitled *On Mrs Priestley Leaving Warrington*, which expressed how much she had loved and enjoyed Mary's company *"whose brightening influence raised my pensive mind"*.[4] It is quite remarkable how many (eight in all) of her poems are inspired by her association with the Priestleys.

Joseph Priestley was proud that he and his wife had been involved in Anna Barbauld's literary career. He rather boasted as much in his *Memoirs* by recording that many of Anna's first poems were written in his house in Leeds during Anna's visits. These poems indicate the breadth of her interest in subjects such as botany, zoology, friendship, industrial development and even politics. Priestley wrote to her from Leeds in 1769 telling her how warmly her poem,

21. John Aikin, brother to Anna. She greatly depended on his judgement and encouragement

Corsica, had been received by Corsican patriots in their struggle for independence from France, and how both he and Mary were *"all expectation at the opening of every packet from Warrington"*.

Her well-known poem, *The Mouse's Petition*, was prompted by a visit to Priestley's house in Leeds. It shows her concern about the need for the humane treatment of animals which was a growing concern in late eighteenth century England, and yet it also suggests that she had reached a more detached stage in her relationship with Priestley. When later published publicly, this playful poem stirred up a popular reaction in the press about the plight of a mouse doomed to suffocate as a result of one of Priestley's experiments with gases. Despite Anna's attempts in subsequent editions to excuse Priestley from any intended cruelty, by associating experimental chemistry with what seemed to be cold and callous behaviour, she had unwittingly fed useful ammunition to his enemies. For example, Thomas Burke (Chapter 10) had Priestley in mind when he later castigated philosophers who *"consider men in their experiments, no more than they do mice in an air pump or in a recipient of mephitic gas"*.[5]

In 1772, her brother John persuaded Anna to publish a collection of her poems and they proved to be very popular with the public, going into four editions in the first year. In the following year she had equal success when she collaborated with her brother on their book of *Miscellaneous Pieces*. In point of fact, Anna wrote most of the pieces; her imagination and humour, and the characteristic lightness of her touch, were in sharp contrast to John's rather ponderous and pedantic style of writing. There is a story that the Whig statesman, Charles Fox, when meeting John Aikin at a dinner party took trouble to praise *Miscellaneous Pieces*. *"I particularly admire"*, said Fox, *"your essay Against Inconsistency in our Expectations"*. *"That"*, answered Aikin, *"is my sister's"*. *"I like much"*, returned Fox, *"your essay On Monastic Institutions"*.

22. A mouse experiment

"*That*", replied Aikin "*is also my sister's*". Fox thought it best to say no more about the essays.[6]

With the publication of her poems and essays Anna soon established a reputation as very promising author. Priestley wrote to her in 1773 welcoming her latest publication and at the same tine informing her about his success in some remarkable experiments on mixing ether with different gases. A literary career certainly beckoned Anna. But she turned her back on fame. She married and, as it was described, "*went to live in the middle of nowhere to run a school for boys*".[7]

Marriage

Among the many students at Warrington who admired Anna Aikin was Rochemont Barbauld. He was the grandson of a French Huguenot who had fled to England, so the story goes, hidden in a cask. Rochemont was sent to the Warrington Academy in 1767 where he soon became a Dissenter. He was six years younger than Anna. Although small and insignificant in appearance, he had an excitable and theatrical manner which seems to have attracted Anna. Lucy Aikin, her niece, later came to describe Anna's eventual attachment to

23. Portrait of Anna Barbauld painted by her husband, Rochemont

Barbauld as *"the illusion of a romantic fancy – not of a tender heart"*.[8] Unfortunately, Rochemont was mentally unstable and Anna was warned that he had already had one attack of insanity. She was urged to break off her engagement but refused on the grounds that to do so would certainly drive him into madness. Nevertheless, right to the very brink of the marriage she wrote openly about her misgivings. With a kind of desperation *"she rushed upon her melancholy destiny"*.[9] However, at least in the early years, the marriage was by all accounts a relatively happy one, and a number of Anna's poems celebrate the love and companionship she and husband were finding together.

School in Suffolk
Within a few months of their marriage in 1774, Anna and Rochemont moved to Palgrave near Diss on the border of Suffolk and Norfolk where Rochemont had been offered a post of minister to the local Dissenting congregation. Both believed strongly in the value of education and they decided to open a boarding school for boys. These were hard and trying times for Anna. Not only was she missing the congenial company of Warrington, she now had to work tirelessly as a teacher and as the main organiser of the school. However, they both had the satisfaction of seeing the school flourish. Anna's reputation as a writer, together with some useful personal connections of Rochemont, helped to attract several of the sons of aristocratic and well-off families to the school.

The school was strong academically – it offered science and modern languages as well as classics – but above all it was a happy one. Anna had already formed some strong ideas about education from discussions she had had with her father, Priestley and the other tutors at the Warrington Academy. Her views were liberal ones, that a child's upbringing and education should be based on an appeal to reason rather than fear, and on the importance of example. Talents were there to be encouraged and the school was well-endowed with theatricals, verse writing and games. Within a short time she was writing to her brother, John: *"Be it known to you, that Palgrave seminary will soon abound with poets, even as the green fields abound with grass hoppers"*.[10] Several of the boys who were taught by the Barbaulds achieved eminence later in their lives, such as Thomas Denman, later Lord Denman and a Lord Chief Justice.

Friction with Priestley
During the 1770s Anna's relationship with Priestley became cooler. Much as she admired him, she was not without criticism of him. They were in fact very different people both in terms of personality and in some of the opinions they held. For a start, although Anna was happy to be associated socially with the Unitarians, she did not share their religious beliefs, once referring to Socinianism (the more extreme form of Unitarianism adopted by Priestley) as *"Christianity in the frigid zone"*.[11] Her attitude to religion was more devotional

than doctrinal, and she looked for warmth and passion in it; its seat, she said, was in the imaginations and the passions. Anna also felt strongly about *"the virtues ascribed to her sex, such as sympathy and affection, sociability and conversation, an innate delicacy of taste"*.[12] One of her strengths as a writer was her ability to present her views with affection, warmth and with respect. Although not sentimental, she was happy to write about sentiment, and she showed delight in ordinary people and events. She had, too, a sense of humour and enjoyed making gentle fun of people and events. For example, her poem, *The Groans of the Tankard*, laments the "luckless day":

Which doomed me to a Presbyterian's power:
Fated to serve the Puritanic race
Whose slender meal is shorter than their grace;
Whose moping sons no jovial orgies keep;
Where evening brings no summons – but to sleep;
No Carnival is even Christmas here,
And one long Lent involves the meagre year.

Priestley, on the other hand, was first and foremost a rationalist, and gave relatively little serious precedence to aesthetics and to what Anna referred to as the *"charms of poetry"*.[13] He claimed that in his early years he was a *"great versifier"*, but when he had encouraged his students to write poetry, it was not to make them into poets but more to improve their writing skills and powers of composition. It has been said that he saw little use for fiction beyond to *"amuse the imagination, and give play to the passions"*.[14] Little wonder Anna felt that her friend's strongly held views posed a threat to her own sensibilities and her dedication to literature. Soon she began to express her criticism of his dry rationalism.

Their differences came to a head in 1775 when Anna published her essay, *Thoughts on the Devotional Taste*. In this work she argued that the language of love was vital to religious devotion *"since its seat is in the imagination and the passions, the vast, and the beautiful"*. She pointed out that *"too critical a spirit is the bane of everything great or pathetic. In our creeds let us be guarded, let us weigh every syllable: but in composition addressed to the heart, let us give freer scope to the language of affections, and the overflowing of a warm and generous disposition"*.[15]

When he read her essay Priestley took umbrage. He seems to have seen her work as being a veiled personal attack on himself. In December 1775 he wrote a frank and forceful letter to Anna from Calne, making it clear that her sentiments were very different from his own. He rejected the importance she had attached to her romantic view of devotion which, he argued, should instead be pious and filial, and more like the *"mixture of love and reverence that a child bears towards his parent"*.[16]

When the essay was reprinted Anna tactfully omitted some of the passages to which Priestley had objected, but she was certainly not dissuaded from her views. We know that Priestley remained upset by her critical remarks. He could not resist linking her with Roman Catholics in holding that *"ignorance is the mother of devotion"*, and accused her of providing cover and comfort to those Dissenters who had defected to the Establishment.[17] We have to wait until the 1790s when Anna defended Priestley against the rising level of intimidation and violence directed against the Dissenters, for the former affection between the two to be fully restored

Writing for Children
Having no children of their own, the Barbaulds in 1777 reached an arrangement with Anna's brother John that they could adopt his third son, Charles, and bring him up as a child of their own. This brought Anna great joy. It was the experience of educating Charles, along with other young children at the Palgrave school, which inspired her to write in 1778/79 one of her most influential books, the four volumes of *Lessons for Children*. The book was designed to help young children to read by drawing on experiences of the world around them in all its variety and richness. It paints a rather rosy picture of nursery life at that time with descriptions of children sliding on ice, snowballing, hay making and gathering fruit. But she did not sentimentalise, explaining things that happened in nature such as cats devouring birds, dogs killing rabbits, and hounds chasing and catching hares and tearing them to pieces.[18]

A short time after Anna published *Hymns in Prose for Children* (1781) which turned out to be an equally popular household work well into the nineteenth century. It went through 30 editions and was published in five languages.

It was not long before Anna ran into criticism from some quarters, such as Charles Fox and Dr Johnson, that she was wasting her talents by writing for children. However, the books were well written and universally popular, and were an important achievement. With justification, Anna can be seen by contemporaries as one of the first serious writers for children. She had appreciated the fact that there were virtually no books designed specifically to stimulate and stretch the imagination and understanding of young children. Books such as *Robinson Crusoe* and *Gulliver's Travels* could be read and enjoyed by children but they were not specifically written for them. Other nursery classics were often based around fables, romances, traditional fairy tales and rhymes. Anna wrote specifically with the needs of the child reader in mind. She insisted that her books were printed in large type with wide margins so that they could be read easily. And most importantly she wrote in a simple informal style which could hold a child's interest. The example set by someone so highly thought of as Anna encouraged other authors to follow suit.

24. Reprint of a page from Barbauld's *Hymns in Prose for Children*. It was a country book whose appeal lasted well over a hundred years

At Palgrave, the Barbaulds enjoyed visiting and receiving friends from nearby Norwich, but Anna loved best her visits in the school holidays to London where she stayed with Rochemont's family in Berwick Street and enjoyed being part of the city's literary circles. This was the one of the high points of Anna's life. Her literary acclaim, her social connections and the success of the Palgrave school meant the future looked bright. But in 1785 the Barbaulds decided suddenly to close their thriving school and to travel abroad for a while. They told their friends that ill health brought upon them by the toil and strain of running the school was the reason, but there is little doubt that Rochemont's increasingly unstable mental condition made it impossible to continue with the responsibility of running the school. Their adopted son Charles, now aged 10, was to be left in England and in the autumn of 1785 they embarked for Calais for a tour of the Continent.

Life in London
On return from their travels in 1786, they soon settled in Hampstead where Rochemont Barbauld had accepted an invitation to become a minister to the Dissenting congregation. They were pleased with their new home. Anna wrote to her brother John that Hampstead was *"certainly the prettiest village about London"*, though she did concede that, *"apart from Avignon it is the most windy place I ever was in"*.[19] The Barbaulds' interest in education remained and they decided to take in a few pupils to teach. Amongst Anna's pupils was Anne

Finch, the granddaughter of Mary and Joseph Priestley. Anne's mother Sally had been abandoned by an improvident husband and left with several small children; her plight was a great worry to the Priestleys. Writing from America later in 1797, Joseph made a point of warmly thanking Anna for taking Sally's daughter under her care.

At Hampstead, Anna was reluctant to take on any literary work but she became increasingly drawn to reviewing and in writing short pieces of work such as pamphlets. The booming publishing industry meant that this was the great age of pamphleteering whereby people could express their opinions on all sorts of matters but especially on public affairs. For someone like Anna, a fluent writer with a lively interest in political and social issues, the pamphlet was the ideal medium.

She quickly became a very accomplished pamphleteer, writing elegantly and deploying where necessary her arguments with sarcasm, irony and ridicule. Her pamphlet in 1790, *An Address to the Opposers of the Repeal of the Corporation and Test Acts*, triggered by the failure of Parliament to repeal the Acts, was particularly scathing and forceful. She also sympathised strongly with the campaign to abolish the slave trade. When in 1791 William Wilberforce's anti-slave trade motion was rejected by Parliament, Anna expressed her deep disappointment in a poem addressed to him, *Epistle on the Rejection of the Bill for Abolishing the Slave Trade*.

In 1791, any past differences Anna may still have had with Joseph Priestley were swept away by the Birmingham riots which forced him and Mary to flee to London. Anna was deeply shocked by the riots. She published anonymously her *Civic Sermons to the People*, a political statement setting out in simple terms her views on the principles of democratic government. Without specifically naming the Priestleys, she led people to think carefully about the events that led to their persecution and denounced the rioters as brutes who deserved to be governed like brutes. Fearlessly, she condemned the King and his supporters for letting the mob loose; and in January 1793 in her poem *To Doctor Priestley*, she turned her wrath on the weakness of those who had failed to come to the support of the embattled Priestley in his hour of need:

> *Stirs not thy spirit, Priestley! As the train*
> *With low obeisance, and with servile phrase,*
> *File behind file, advance, with supple knee,*
> *And lay their necks beneath the foot of power?*
> *Burns not thy cheek indignant, when thy name,*
> *On which delighted Sciences loved to dwell,*
> *Becomes the bandied theme of hooting crowds?*[20]

In this scornful poem, Anna seems also to have understood that Priestley's work in England was probably at an end, and that if the fight for religious and civil liberty was to be won, the torch now had to pass to others who should draw strength from his writings and the memories of him.

The riots did at least offer the consolation of Anna becoming re-united with Mary and Joseph for a while once more. The Priestleys lived at Clapton in London for three years whilst Joseph served as a tutor at the Hackney New College. Once more she was able to enjoy their company, and just for a short time *"the spirit of Warrington was abroad"*.[21] But Priestley became more and more depressed as abuse and threats continued to be hurled at him. He and Mary felt distinctly unsafe and the decision to emigrate was taken in the summer of 1793.

Anna and Priestley continued to correspond but their letters had a sad note. When Mary Priestley died in America three years after leaving England, Joseph felt the loss deeply and he wrote to Anna asking whether she might still have any copies of her early poems relating to his wife and to the happy days at the Warrington Academy. He knew how important the friendship between Mary and Anna had been, and declared *"there were not many persons who were more frequently the subject of our conversation, or whom she spoke of with so much pleasure as yourself"*.[22] He went on to regret that his early diaries had been destroyed in the Birmingham riots. Unfortunately, Mary had personally also destroyed her papers at about the same time as a precaution against them falling into the wrong hands, together with a folio book in which she had copied all Anna's unpublished poems, and which included the first poem she wrote to Mary when the Priestleys left the Academy. In 1798 Priestley wrote again to Anna saying how much *"I should value that above any other; and also the little poem you wrote on the birth of Joseph"*.[23] He also expressed his gratitude to Anna for the kindness she was showing in England to his daughter Sally whose trials were very great in the face of the *"strange obstinacy and prejudice"* of her husband Mr Finch.

Stoke Newington
Anna was very fond of her brother John and continued to collaborate with him on several publications. When ill health forced him to retire from his medical practice and move to the then village of Stoke Newington in north London, Anna decided that she wanted to be closer to him, especially as the mental stability of her husband was becoming increasingly worrying. An opportunity arose in 1802 when the Presbyterian community in Stoke Newington offered Rochemont the post of minister of their chapel.

Anna's gift for friendship helped her to settle in quickly to her new home but her mood was depressed and she wrote little there at first. To some extent her spirits were restored when she was asked produce an edition of letters of the early eighteenth century writer, Samuel Richardson. But she was clearly distressed by the mental problems of her husband; Rochemont's illness was characterised by a love/hate relationship with Anna and he said that he could neither live with or without her. The tragedy was that his antipathy could quickly turn to violence and her life was in great danger. At dinner one day he clasped a knife and chased her around the table and she escaped only by jumping out of the window.[24] Anna continued to resist attempts by her family to leave her husband but she finally agreed to a separation. Tragically, in 1808 Rochemont bribed his manservant to let him go out alone and he drowned himself in a nearby river.

Anna grieved deeply for her husband and sought consolation in her writing. In addition to writing regularly for the *Monthly Review* to which she contributed over 300 articles over six years, she forced herself in 1810 to edit a giant edition in 50 volumes of *The British Novelists*. She also turned once more to writing poetry but this time with calamitous results. Her long epic poem *Eighteen Hundred and Eleven* reflects her despondent mood, heightened by her despair over the endless Napoleonic wars. In the poem she denounced Britain for lending support to repressive regimes as allies in the war with France and portrayed Europe in sad and terminal decline. She saw hope for civilisation only in America where "*the Genius of the Earth Leaves the Old World for the New*". She closed the poem with the words, "*Thy world, Columbus, shall be free*".[25]

Not surprisingly the poem provoked a very angry and bitter response especially from the Tory press. Even some of her friends were critical but the most personal and scathing attack came in the influential *Quarterly Review* by a reviewer called John Wilson Croker. After ridiculing her argument, Croker concluded by "*entreating her, with great earnestness, that she would not, for the sake of this ungrateful generation, put herself to the trouble of writing any more part pamphlets in verse*".[26]

Friends tried to console her, but deeply hurt by the hostile reception to her poem, she published virtually nothing more. She still took great trouble to encourage young poets, many of whom admired her writing and she had the comfort of her friends and family. But she became more melancholic, especially after her beloved brother John Aikin died in 1822. Nonetheless, she bore her final years with that quiet stoicism and serenity characteristic of Dissenters of her time. For some years she had suffered from asthma which became progressively worse and she died at her home in March 1825. She was buried beside her husband in the Presbyterian Cemetery in Newington Green. On her death Anna Barbauld received many tributes to her character, the quality of her mind and her attainments. The author, Maria Edgeworth, wrote that "*England had lost a great writer and we a most sincere friend*".[27]

Conclusion

During Anna Barbauld's lifetime, Britain had changed greatly. By the time of her death the battles of the late eighteenth century in which the Dissenters had played a leading role were over. The Test and Corporation Acts were repealed in 1828. The fears and controversies ignited by the American War of Independence and the French Revolution had subsided. The slave trade had been abolished. The Age of Reason gave way to that of the Romantic Movement. Anna had a foot in both the past and the new worlds.

She never abandoned her cool, elegant and logically assertive style, one that came to irritate the later Romantics like Coleridge who cruelly dubbed her *"Mistress Bare and Bold"*. She may have resisted the wilder excesses of the later Romantics, but she deservedly justifies the description of her as one of the first Romantics in the way she turned to writing about the world around her, and to nature, and to expressing her innermost feelings in a spontaneous and individual way. She showed courage and independence of thought in challenging political, social and education conditions, as well as the conventions of the day.

Both Joseph and Mary Priestley must take credit for nurturing Anna's talents in her early years. They gave her the confidence to express her feelings publicly in an age when women were still expected to confine themselves to 'safe' topics such as love, domesticity and religion, and not to enter the public domain. As she matured, the sensibility of her personality, and devotion to the world of the arts and nature, ran counter to the cool rationality of the scientist Priestley, but the underlying respect and affection for each other's virtues never wavered.

CHAPTER 6

Theophilus Lindsey
(1723–1808)
The Closest Friend

Theophilus Lindsey was an influential and controversial clergyman of the eighteenth century. Regarded by many as destined to reach the highest levels of the Church of England, he shocked Georgian society by abandoning his career to play a significant part in establishing the Unitarian Church in Britain.

Lindsey was arguably the truest and closest friend of Joseph Priestley. In his memoirs, Priestley described his introduction to Lindsey as one of the blessings of his life. It was a deep personal and intellectual friendship lasting 35 years until Priestley's death in 1804. Each drew inspiration and strength from it and they achieved much together. Priestley hoped that his own name *"may ever be connected with yours after death, as we have been connected by friendship in life"*.[1]

25. Theophilus Lindsey

Lindsey came from a different background from Priestley and had a somewhat different temperament. He was an earnest, sincere and reserved man who preferred to shun controversy. He chose not to discuss political issues from the pulpit or in public and showed more discretion than Priestley. However, his tongue could be sharp at times and in private he enjoyed the cut and thrust of argument. He was liberal in politics and had the same fierce regard as Priestley for the search for truth. He disliked ostentatious piety and was more of a *"practical Christian, not merely a desiccated theorist"*.[2] He engaged actively in philanthropic works and he and his wife took much pleasure in organising Sunday schools. He was a clear, exact and methodical thinker, but not particularly an original one, and did not attempt to compete with Priestley's intellectual range.

Early Life
Born at Middlewich in Cheshire in 1723, Lindsey was the youngest son of a Scottish businessman. He quickly showed promise. From Leeds Grammar School he went up to St John's College, Cambridge where he was subsequently appointed a Fellow. However, he resisted attempts to persuade him to pursue an academic career, and decided to commit his life to the Church of England. He was ordained a minister in 1746. His high character and academic success attracted attention, not least in aristocratic circles, and he took up an appointment as private chaplain to the Duke of Somerset, and as a tutor to the future Duke of Northumberland. He spent some time travelling on the Continent before becoming minister of a modest parish at Kirby-Wiske near Richmond in Yorkshire.

It was there that he met and became friendly with the clergyman who was to have a powerful influence on his own spiritual development – Francis Blackburne, the Archdeacon of Cleveland. The Archdeacon had developed over the years serious doubts about the requirement for all Anglican clergymen to subscribe by law to the Thirty Nine Articles and to all the liturgy of the Church of England. These doubts were to be publicly aired in 1766 when Blackburne published anonymously his important book entitled *The Confessional*. In his book he argued that Protestant Churches had no right to set up creeds which had been composed by men rather than in accordance with the Word of God, and then to use them as tests for orthodox ministers. Therefore, he reasoned, clerical subscription to the Thirty Nine Articles of Religion should be abolished.

Predictably, the book stirred up considerable hostility among conservatives who maintained that unless all its members fully subscribed to the Articles, the Anglican Church would fall apart. However the book also won a lot of approval and influence. It led eventually to the organised movement to launch an appeal to Parliament in 1772 to get relief from subscription to the Articles which became known as the *Feathers' Tavern Petition* since it was drawn up at a public house in London. Lindsey was to play a prominent part in drafting the document.

After three years at Richmond, Lindsey accepted the post of minister to a parish in Dorset where he spent the next seven years as a very popular and conscientious priest. It was there that he married the stepdaughter of Archdeacon Blackburne, Hannah Elsworth. He and his wife returned to Yorkshire in 1763 when he took up a new post in the parish of Catterick, a fairly prosperous church living. Lindsey's own doubts about the requirement to subscribe to all the Articles were now even stronger. He was moreover deeply troubled by the fact that his study of the Bible had convinced him he should worship God alone, rather than offer worship to Christ and the Holy Spirit which the Anglican Prayer Book required him to do. As a consequence, he moved closer to the Unitarian position.

Meeting with Priestley
Lindsey seems to have first met Joseph Priestley through mutual friends in the late 1760s when Priestley was minister at the Mill Hill Chapel, Leeds. The friendship quickly deepened and Lindsey used his influence to persuade some of his aristocratic connections to help resource Priestley's scientific experiments. At the time, although Priestley shared Lindsey's qualms about the divinity of Christ, he did not yet call himself a Unitarian. Later in the summer of 1769 at a meeting at Archdeacon Blackburne's house, Lindsey confided his serious religious doubts to Priestley and told him of his intention of resigning his church living. Priestley, somewhat out of character, counselled him to stay put and keep a low profile; he advised him to modify his stance towards those passages in the Prayer Book which Lindsey found unacceptable, and wait to see how his Bishop reacted. Since Lindsey was deeply aware that as a priest he had solemnly promised to use the Church's liturgy, a man of his conscience was unlikely to find Priestley's advice easy to accept. He redoubled his work among the poor of Catterick, supplying them with food, medicines and books, but openly and bravely continued to express his religious views with the hope of getting some concessions from the Church. But this was not to be.

When the *Feathers' Tavern* movement gathered pace around 1770, Lindsey recognised that it represented possibly his last chance of finding a way to stay in the Church of England. He knew the chances of change were slim but embarked on an energetic personal campaign to collect as many signatures as possible in support of the Petition. He is said to have travelled on horseback some 2,000 miles through winter rain and snow to find signatures. He was encouraged by some early success – the Master of Jesus College, Cambridge and the entire resident Fellows signed the petition – but he soon found that many of the clergy who privately professed sympathy for the Petition were later reluctant to sign through fear of the consequences for their careers. The Rev. William Paley, later

26. Priestley, Lindsey and Price campaign for the repeal of the Test and Corporation Acts to a sceptical audience

a famous theologian, summed up the feelings of many when he declined to sign because *"he could not afford to keep a conscience"*.[3] Lindsey later complained that he had lived to see four clergymen who had encouraged him, and then drew back, eventually raised to the episcopate. In total he only obtained around 250 signatures. The Petition was presented to Parliament in 1772 but it was opposed strongly by orthodox Anglicans and the Methodists. After a stormy eight hour debate, Parliament refused even to receive it.

The Break with the Church
Consequently, Lindsey decided that the time had finally come to leave the Church of England. He resigned his living and withdrew from the Church on 12 November 1773. He informed Blackburne and other friends of the reasons for his decision and published them fully in his *Apology for Resigning the Vicarage of Catterick*. He wrote an affectionate Farewell Address to his parishioners and preached a final sermon to them.

Lindsey was a man of 50 when he resigned. He had given up a comfortable living and was in poor health. He faced a totally unknown future. After selling all but his most precious possessions he had around £50 to his name. And sadly when he needed them most, he found many of his former church friends deserting him. Even his father-in-law, Archdeacon Blackburne, refused to see Lindsey and his wife for several years. Some of the Feathers' Tavern petitioners accused Lindsey that his resignation had weakened the chances of eventual success for their cause. His wife, Hannah, however, who shared his religious views, stood resolutely beside him, and indignantly refused an outrageous offer from a wealthy relation to provide for her if she would abandon her husband.

Others outside the Anglican Church were more sympathetic to Lindsey's predicament and various offers of work were made to him from Dissenting organisations. Lindsey declined them all. He was reluctant to sever all his ties with the Anglican Church, believing, in the event naively, that there were many people like him who valued the Church of England and hoped that in time it would itself make the important changes they wanted to see in its liturgy. He resolved to try and create in London a congregation for people of that persuasion. On reaching the city he and his wife took lodgings in two scantily furnished rooms, and thereupon set about the task of reforming the Anglican liturgy by drawing up a revised Prayer Book. His work – *A Liturgy, Altered from that of the Church of England, to suit Unitarian Doctrine* – by setting out clearly Unitarian objections to the Anglican Church, provided the foundation for later Unitarian forms of worship. However if Lindsey's primary purpose was to reform the Church of England from within he was unsuccessful. Very few Anglican clergymen were prepared to subscribe fully to the changes he advocated.

Priestley much admired Lindsey for his honesty and the courage and sacrifice he had shown in resigning from his living. He was determined to do what he could to assist him to start a fresh life. With the help of his influential friend Dr Richard Price (Chapter 3) and other liberal Dissenters, enough funds were raised for Lindsey to rent a vacant auction room in Essex Street, off the Strand in London, and for it to be fitted out as a suitable place of worship. On 17 April

27. The Essex Street Chapel as it was at the Centenary Meeting in 1874. The Chapel became popular with the well-connected and liberal religious people of London

1774 the Essex Street Chapel opened as the first place of worship in England which was to be run explicitly according to Unitarian principles.

At the first service about 200 people were present, including Priestley, Benjamin Franklin and a government agent whose job it was to keep an eye on things. For his text, Lindsey chose Ephesians 4:3, *"Endeavouring to keep the unity of the Spirit in the bond of peace"*. However, the Chapel faced a precarious future since it was still against the law to deny the Trinity, and Lindsey was careful to satisfy the authorities that he had no intention of engaging in religious controversy. In practice, the actual services conducted were kept quite similar to those of the Church of England, apart from the use of the Lindsey's Revised Prayer Book and the fact that the minister wore no surplice.

Although the average congregation was never large, the Chapel soon established itself as an important meeting place for discussing not only Unitarian ideas but liberal Dissenting policies in general. Many notable and influential people are known to have attended including Sir George Saville, who was one of the two county MPs for Yorkshire, Sir Thomas Brand, the treasurer of the Foundling Hospital, the scientist Richard Kirwan, FRS, and the Earl of Surrey.

Lindsey would have been prepared to stay out of the limelight and to keep clear of controversy. However, he was not allowed to do so. There were many in the Church of England who were offended by the path he had taken and lost no time in attacking him for his action and beliefs. Even the relative success of the Essex Street Chapel was resented and used to accuse him of resigning from the Church in order to make more money! Reluctantly, Lindsey felt compelled openly to declare his Unitarian beliefs, and to answer publicly the attacks being made on him.

Lindsey and Priestley

During this difficult period, the personal encouragement and reassurance provided by friends and supporters were hugely important for Lindsey. Several of Lindsey's letters express his admiration for Priestley and how much he depended on him. He remarked to a friend, *"One is never tired of being with him"*.[4] His discussions with Priestley over issues of scripture and theology gave him the inspiration and confidence to develop and express his own non-orthodox views more cogently. With Priestley's help he began openly to publish his theological works. In his *Historical View of Unitarianism* (1783) Lindsey firmly placed the Unitarian movement not as a sect, but as nearly as old as Protestantism, and one which had attracted eminent followers over many years and in several countries.

Priestley, too, benefited considerably from their friendship. Lindsey had managed to keep some of his influential and well-off friends, and he encouraged them to help Priestley in his various activities, especially with equipment for his scientific work. He also openly defended Priestley as far as he could from the same type of vituperative attacks he himself had to endure. At that very low point of Priestley's life following the Birmingham riots, when several of his friends abandoned him, it was Lindsey who resolutely stood by him. The scientist it was said, *"found a refuge in his Lindsey's arms"*.[5]

Perhaps most significant of all was the help Lindsey gave to Priestley as a counsellor and critical friend. By the late 1770s, Priestley had adopted the habit of submitting his more important written work for Lindsey to vet before publication. He admitted that *"I never chose to publish any thing of moment relating to theology, without consulting him"*.[6] This served Priestley very well since he was a hasty writer and reluctant to spend time on revising or correcting his work. Lindsey was more patient and methodical. He became adept at pointing out to his friend where there were errors or pieces of work where the reasoning was unclear or unsound.

Lindsey had moreover a political sensitivity which Priestley too rashly overlooked or rejected. Lindsey appreciated just how prominent and controversial a public figure his friend had become by the mid-1770s. He was rightly apprehensive that Priestley's more extreme views would not only provoke the authorities, but damage both the cause of Dissenters in general, and of Unitarians in particular. He was therefore careful to warn Priestley about the use of words and phrases that his enemies would be only too pleased to turn against him.

For the most part Priestley accepted the advice and corrections of his friend but that was not always the case. When Priestley was convinced that an important principle or misinterpretation was at stake, then nothing would deflect him from expressing himself openly and forcefully, and with little apparent concern for the consequences. We know for example that Priestley in 1784 resumed his work on his controversial *Theological Repository*, which dealt among other things with his views on the development of the character of Christ. When the draft was presented to Lindsey for review he became very alarmed that the questions discussed in the work would stir up further controversy and *"increase the prejudices of multitudes against him and hinder others less indisposed from reading his works"*.[7] Whilst Priestley gave careful attention to his friend's criticisms on this occasion, he did not entirely modify his views.

Both men also worked hard together to promote the fortunes of the Essex Street Chapel, as well as the cause of the Unitarian movement generally across the country. Where possible they shared the preaching load. Priestley delivered some notable sermons at the Essex Street Chapel, much admired by Lindsey for their style and substance. By all accounts Lindsey was not himself a particularly inspiring preacher, and reluctant to do so outside his own Chapel, but on occasions he preached for Priestley at the New Meeting House in Birmingham, to students at Oxford and Cambridge and elsewhere. Both proved excellent ambassadors for the Unitarian movement and helped to make many distinguished converts. Among them was Augustus Henry Fitzroy, 3rd Duke of Grafton, a former prime minister and Chancellor of Cambridge University, who became a lifelong supporter of Priestley.

The Farewell
The decision Priestley took in 1794 to follow his sons and emigrate to America came as a grievous blow to Lindsey although it was not unexpected. Lindsey's good sense told him that his friend was making the right decision. Priestley and his family were simply no longer safe in London, and as much as Lindsey might counsel prudence, he had come to accept that his friend would continue to attract hostility. Writing to a friend, Lindsey remarked that Priestley's departure would, *"cut off a great source of the highest satisfaction to me, amongst many others. But ... I have for some time thought that his chief business was done here, and we were no longer worthy of him, and that he will be of eminent service to that other country"*.[8] It was a heavy-hearted occasion, too, for Priestley. On 6 April 1794 he attended the Essex Street Chapel for the last time. Many of those present were close friends whom he would never see again. This saddened him, but it was the loss of his friend Lindsey that he felt the most, *"In whose absence"*, he said, *"I shall for some time at least find the entire world a blank"*.[9]

Through a continuous stream of letters, the two men kept in touch until Priestley's death in 1804. In all, we know that Priestley wrote over 100 letters from America to his friend. In the main, they reflected Priestley's preoccupation with political and religious issues for he was not one to dwell on the personal and domestic aspects of his life in his new country. The letters do, however, reflect his feeling of isolation and how much he was missing his friends and none more so than Lindsey. The personal bond between the two men remained deep and they were always concerned about each other's health and well-being. Lindsey had suffered a severe stroke in December 1801 but he was soon strong enough to pen a short postscript in a letter to Priestley from Mrs Lindsey. Priestley was overjoyed to hear of his friend's recovery; *"The few lines"*, he replied, that his friend had added with his own hand, *"quite overcame me: and if I read them, as I shall do, a hundred times, I shall have the same emotions. Such friendship as his and yours has been to me can never be exceeded on this side of the grave"*.[10]

Lindsey had retired from the pulpit in 1793 at the age of 70. He published only one more book but remained always ready to advise and support the Unitarian cause, and had the satisfaction of seeing his views spread widely in the British Isles, and, at least in the early days, in the New England region of America. Priestley, who at the time enjoyed reasonably good health, might have been expected to outlive his friend who was ten years older than him. When nearly 70, he told Lindsey that he was by far his principal acquaintance, and added *"Should I survive you, the world will appear to me a dreary waste"*.[11] However, it was Priestley who died first in February 1804. Lindsey was to survive for another four years and died in the eighty-sixth year of his life. It is said that his last rational words were *"God's will is done"*.[12]

Conclusion

When Lindsey left the Anglican Church in 1773 after 30 years as an exemplary parish priest, his main intention was to establish in effect a denomination within a wider and more tolerant Church of England. In the event his life had little impact on the Anglican Church and when it came to the point few of the clergy followed him. His hopes disappointed, compensation for Lindsey came from the perfect friendship, which in the space of a relatively few years he formed with Joseph Priestley. Between them they were to make a remarkable contribution to the development of the Unitarian movement.

Their success rested much on the character of the two men. The quiet, studious, judicious Lindsey was the perfect foil to the bold, impetuous and fiercely committed Priestley. In effect, Lindsey provided the Unitarian church with its code of religious practice and organisation while Priestley developed its theology and influence. Within a few years the Essex Street Chapel under their direction and inspiration became most influential, and a model for others elsewhere. Importantly, the inspiration offered by the two men and their example gave courage to other Dissenters who had gradually drifted, rather apprehensively, into Unitarian views. In 1789 there were just two Unitarian churches in London; by 1810 there were 20 or so.

Both men would not have judged their friendship simply in terms of accomplishments, important as they were. It meant more than that to both of them, for at bottom it was based on the values and beliefs they shared, and on the recognition of the moral goodness of each another.

CHAPTER 7

Antoine Lavoisier
(1743–1794)
The Father of Modern Chemistry

In the latter half of the eighteenth century, two exceptional scientists were at work. They hardly ever met, and yet in the history of science the lives of the two men have become inextricably linked. In England Joseph Priestley was making a series of discoveries that astonished the scientific world. In the space of a few years he discovered no less than nine new gases. In France, the aristocratic and very different scientist, Antoine Lavoisier, was wrestling with a new scientific approach that would lay the foundation for the chemistry we know today. In the 1770s, these two men, though not fully aware of it, engaged in experiments leading to the discovery of perhaps the most important gas of all – oxygen. There is still debate over two centuries on as to which scientist should be hailed as the true discoverer; indeed there is a third contender, the Swedish pharmacist Carl Wilhelm Scheele. Their encounter has all the makings of an epic drama. It is not surprising that it has recently become the subject of a play written by two Nobel Laureate chemists.[1]

The approach of Priestley and Lavoisier to scientific investigation was quite different. Priestley was primarily a theologian, who believed that the study of science would provide further understanding of God's grand design on earth. Lavoisier dedicated his life to science and searched to explain the world without any intervention of divine providence. Priestley was an outstanding investigator who never claimed to be a theorist although he was meticulous in his preparation and recording. He liked to gather together all the information and then begin the task of making sense of it. In a reference to his work on the discovery of oxygen, he said that *"it provides a striking illustration of a remark I have more than once made in my philosophical writings . . . that more is owing to what we call chance . . . than any proper design or preconceived theory"*.

Lavoisier took the opposite or the modern approach to scientific investigation. He rarely experimented by chance. He proposed a hypothesis first, and then searched for evidence to complete the chain of thought, thereby reconciling apparently discordant facts into the framework of an orderly theory. Applying

28. Lavoisier with his wife Marie-Anne

this approach enabled Lavoisier to change chemistry from a qualitative to a quantitative science and he is justly regarded by many as the Father of Modern Chemistry.

There were important differences too in how they liked to communicate. Priestley was a straightforward, affable character who liked to share with others the excitement and results of his experiments, and how he went about them. He was not a competitive scientist and embodied the Enlightenment ideal that truth should be open to all and kept as understandable as possible. As a committed educator, he wanted to make people think for themselves and enjoyed the opportunity to recount his discoveries in full and colourful detail to a wide range of audiences.

Lavoisier was the more complex man. He could be kind and sincere, but on the other hand to others he often seemed cold, vain and ruthlessly ambitious. Very rational, he was determined to overcome what he regarded as the dogma and imprecision of the old science. It was said that, *"Lavoisier has no need of the philosopher's stone, he has found it in his job"*.[2] There was none of the light-heartedness that we can find in Priestley's scientific writings. He was a wholly serious scientist and with the wealth to pursue his researches relentlessly. He was, in truth, a professional compared to the amateur; he once remarked on Priestley's work as consisting *"more or less of experiments, almost uninterrupted by any reasoning, an assembly of facts"*.[3]

His Life

Lavoisier was the son of a wealthy Parisian lawyer. He studied law but never practised as he was far more interested in science and mathematics. At the very early age of 25 he was elected in 1768 to the *Académie des Sciences*, France's elite scientific society, mainly for his work on providing lighting for the streets of Paris. In the same year he took what was to prove later to be a fatal step by buying into the *Ferme Générale*, a private corporation that collected taxes of all kinds for the Crown. Unfortunately, it had acquired a reputation for corruption and it was an organisation hated by merchants and the peasantry. However, there is no evidence that Lavoisier himself ever behaved dishonestly in carrying out his duties. He married in 1771 Marie-Anne Pierette Paulze, a farmer's daughter when she was not quite 14. This remarkable women devoted her life to helping her husband in his scientific work and was his chief collaborator; she even learned English (which Lavoisier never did) so as to translate the work of British chemists, especially that of Priestley.

In 1775, Lavoisier became a Commissioner of the Royal Gunpowder and Saltpetre administration. With the funds provided for him, he attracted able assistants and built up a superb laboratory in which he succeeded in producing more and better gunpowder – the best stock in Europe. He was not particularly religious but had liberal political views and supported the idea of a constitutional monarchy. Interested in economic and social reform, he headed several public commissions requiring scientific investigations on how to improve French agriculture and industry and the lot of the workers and peasants. He drew up plans for the metric system of weights and measures. He eventually became the Director of the prestigious *Académie des Sciences*.

However, like many other leading thinkers of his age he inevitably became embroiled in politics, and despite all his good works and scientific achievements he fell victim to the French Revolution. As the Revolution intensified he had come under attack for his earlier position as a *Fermier Générale*, i.e. a collector of taxes. Imprisoned, and forced to undergo a mockery of a trial, he was guillotined in 1794. As a prominent mathematician of the time put it: "*It took them only an instant to cut off that head, and 100 years may not produce another like it*".[4]

Lavoisier is universally recognised today as a great scientist, who made many fundamental contributions to the science of chemistry. By deploying a quantitative approach to the study of chemistry he brought it into the modern age. In order to make careful measurements of the reactants and products of his experiments, he invented a balance that was accurate to about 0·0005 grams. He was the first to explain definitively the formation of acids and salts. He explained the respiration of animals and plants and the composition of water. He developed a system of chemical nomenclature in use ever since. And importantly, his researches led to the overthrow of the prevailing scientific theory of phlogiston – the theory that was at the heart of his acrimonious and lengthy clash with Joseph Priestley.

The Phlogiston Theory
For the greater part of the eighteenth century virtually all advanced scientists believed that *phlogiston* was a substance without colour, odour, taste or weight that was given off when metals and other combustible substances were burnt. Equally, it was thought that when some metal oxides were heated with charcoal they turned back to metals because the phlogiston-rich charcoal released its phlogiston back into the metal. Since it could not be detected by the senses, phlogiston was regarded as something of a mystical property and akin to caloric (heat) and electricity. There were problems with the theory but at the time none, including Priestley, was involved in accurate measurements in chemistry, so the concept of phlogiston was the accepted theory of the day.

Although it seems far-fetched to modern senses, Priestley was a strong believer in the existence of the theory and interpreted all his experiments with gases in terms of phlogiston. The main problem with the theory was that it did not really explain how things burnt nor why, after the burning of some materials, the weight of the resulting calx (now known as oxide) was greater than it had been before combustion. Supporters of the theory tried to explain this by saying that in some substances phlogiston had a negative weight. Lavoisier on the other hand, could not accept the theory that phlogiston could variously have a positive and negative property, and sometimes no weight at all, and he eventually developed his revolutionary *Antiphlogistic Theory*. In essence this was really the reverse of the phlogistonists' ideas, namely that something material was actually absorbed when combustion took place and this, as Lavoisier proved later, is the gas he named oxygen.

Oxygen
It always gave Priestley great pleasure to recount the story of how he first made his great discovery of what he termed *dephlogisticated air* in his laboratory at Lord Shelburne's mansion near Calne. All his experiments so far had led him to believe that common air itself was made up of several gases of some kind. (In Priestley's time different gases were known as different types of air.) In June 1774, he had acquired a much more powerful burning lens for focusing sunlight which enabled him to improve his experiments. In the following August, he conducted his famous experiment by heating mercury in the presence of common air, and thereby forming the red powder, mercuric oxide. This powder fascinated Priestley, since he was aware that when burnt it released a gas. Earlier scientists such as Robert Boyle had noted the same phenomenon but they had left it at that. When Priestley reheated the oxide it reformed mercury by what Priestley thought was the re-absorption of phlogiston from the surrounding

common air and it was this substance which he then carefully collected. It must be therefore, he concluded, *common air* which had been in effect *dephlogisticated*.

Priestley was very surprised when a candle burned splendidly in the *new air* which he had collected and was at a loss to account for it. Further experiments confirmed the results of the first. Moreover, those conducted with mice present showed that the *new air* seemed in fact much superior to ordinary air. Priestley decided to test it on himself. His record was momentous. He noted that the feeling in his lungs was not sensibly different from that of common air but *"I fancied that my breast felt peculiarly light and easy for some time afterwards. Who can tell but that, in time, this pure air may become a fashionable article in luxury ... Hitherto only my mice and myself have had the privilege of breathing it"*.[5]

Much against his religious convictions, Priestley was forced to admit there was in fact a better *air*, *"five or six times better"* than that provided by nature.

Priestley knew that he had made an important discovery but was unable to make that intellectual leap to break free from the past. He was still entangled with the phlogiston theory. His great error was his failure to name his discovery as something new, something truly different, and he lamely settled for the term *dephlogisticated air*. As a consequence of further experimentation, Priestley went on to conclude that common air was a mixture of one fifth *deplogisticated air* and four fifths *phlogisticated air*.

Priestley Meets Lavoisier

Shortly after the discovery of his new gas in 1774, Priestley accompanied his patron, Lord Shelburne, on a tour of Flanders, Holland and Germany. Priestley was excited by the tour as he had never before travelled abroad and he welcomed the opportunity offered to make the acquaintance of some of the leading continental scientists whose work he had read and commented upon. Although he was received with great respect, in practice, the tour did not quite live up to his expectations. By the time they finally reached Paris, the modest, stuttering Priestley had come to dislike having to attend with Shelburne the succession of opulent dinners and social events. He begged to be excused from them and to be allowed to spend more of his time with scientists and philosophers. Even their company was to prove wearisome and it was not long before Priestley admitted that *"I am quite tired of the idleness in which I spend my time here and long exceedingly to be about my experiments"*.[6]

He was also much put out by the fact that most of the prominent persons to whom he was introduced in Paris were not Christians and more likely to be professed atheists. At one dinner, he was shocked to be told that the two men sitting opposite to him – the Bishop of Aix and the Archbishop of Toulouse –

were *"no more believers than you or I"*. When Priestley retorted that he was a believer, his companion protested in astonishment that, *"no man of science can truly believe in God"*.[7]

Priestley would have met Lavoisier soon after his arrival in Paris and before long he became a regular guest at the French scientist's impressive mansion where particularly lavish dinners were held. On one occasion he was witness to a spectacular experiment which involved to his *"great astonishment the rapid production of... near two gallons of air from a mixture of spirits of nitre and spirit of wine"*.[8] Soon after another grand dinner was held at the Lavoisier table in October 1774 which was to become critically important to the controversy as to which man should have the credit for arguably the greatest scientific discovery of the century.

The dinner was well attended by all the principal philosophers and scientists of the city, and Priestley was the principal attraction. Word had got around Paris about his mysterious *new air* and they were eager to discuss it with him. When asked to describe the discovery of his new gas, Priestley recounted the events in a dramatic fashion, and in broken French, to the spellbound audience. At the end of his discourse he declared, *"It was a kind of air in which a candle burned much better than in common air, but that I had not then given it any name. At this all the company, and Mr and Mrs Lavoisier as much as any, expressed great surprise"*.[9] In later years, Priestley took pains to remind the world about the actual events of this dinner and the fact that he had indeed frequently mentioned his new gas whilst in Paris.

No one had listened more eagerly to Priestley's revelation at the dinner than Lavoisier and his wife, Marie-Anne. Lavoisier had for sometime suspected that there was something in atmospheric air that was added to a metal during combustion but had no proof. He recognised the uniqueness of Priestley's discovery and surmised correctly that it held the key to his own preoccupation with the theory of combustion. Over the next year or two he decided to concentrate his experiments on Priestley's discovery of so-called deplogisticated air.

Controversy Begins

On 23 March 1775 Priestley sent a letter to Sir John Pringle, Secretary of the Royal Society, announcing his discovery of his new gas, which was read out to members later in the month. Soon after, in Paris on 26 April 1775, Lavoisier also made known his research findings in a *Memoir* to the *Académie des Sciences*, affirming that he had isolated a component of air which he called *"eminently breathable air"*. Neither scientist at that time was apparently aware of what the other had reported, but Lavoisier lost no time in ensuring that his work was published in the learned magazine the *Journal de Physique* in May 1775. The results of Priestley's work were published formally only later in

November of that year in the second volume of his book entitled *Experiments and Observations on Different Kinds of Air*.

When Priestley was first shown Lavoisier's *Memoir*, his indignation rose because he could find no acknowledgement of his own name or experiments with the new gas. As Priestley's own research manuscript was still in draft, he used the opportunity to use it to remind his fellow scientist of the ethics of scientific research and to express his displeasure at Lavoisier's lapse. Priestley's principal priority was to ensure that all his readers were made fully aware of the disclosure he had made in October 1774 to the guests at the Lavoisier dinner. Priestley alluded to the shortcomings of his fellow scientist; he drew attention to the fact that during the course of making his own discovery of dephlogisticated air, he was *"not conscious of having concealed the least hint that was suggested to me by any person whatsoever"*.[10] He also took the opportunity to point out some of the experimental errors that Lavoisier had made, which he claimed would convince Lavoisier of the *"imperfection"* of his work.

On other occasions, Priestley expressed his sense of grievance much more frankly. Writing to Thomas Henry, the publisher of Lavoisier's work, he made it plain that the scientist *"ought to have acknowledged that my giving him an account of the air I had got from mercury calc . . . led him to try what air it yielded, which he did after I left"*.[11]

The problem for Lavoisier was that this was not the first time that he had been criticised for not giving sufficient credit to the work of his fellow scientists, even to the extent of plagiarism. He had, for example, very recently been forced to make a public apology for not mentioning the rival discoveries of two Italian chemists in 1774. But matters had become more serious since the complaint against him was now coming from one of the world's foremost scientists – Joseph Priestley. Consequently, the differences between the two men became an international *cause célèbre*; their relationship was never the same again and soon deteriorated into outright animosity.

Lavoisier was fully aware of Priestley's displeasure but was never able to bring himself to apologise to him. In 1776 he did acknowledge grudgingly that:

Perhaps, strictly speaking, there is nothing in it which Mr Priestley would not be able to claim the original idea; but since the same facts have conducted us to diametrically opposite results, I trust that if I am reproached for having borrowed the proofs of the works of this celebrated philosopher, my right at least to the conclusions will not be contested.[12]

Lavoisier simply could not accept that he had no claim to the discovery of the very gas on which rested his whole new theory of combustion. In his famous work *Traite Élémentaire de Chimie* published in 1789 – the first modern chemistry textbook – he described the preparation of oxygen in detail by heating red oxide of mercury and referred explicitly to oxygen as "*this air, which Mr Priestley, Mr Scheele, and I discovered about the same time*".[13]

It is possible that Lavoisier might have been prepared at least to concede Priestley should be given priority, as long as he was also recognised as an independent discoverer. However, history has denied him even that distinction. He can justly claim to have named the new gas, to understand it and realise its importance to the world, but he did not discover oxygen. As for Priestley, although he would never have to share the honour for the discovery of oxygen with the Frenchman, he does now with a Swedish chemist. Records have come to light to show that the self-effacing scientist, Carl Wilhelm Scheele, must also be given equal credit for the discovery in the early 1770s. Scheele had posted a letter to Lavoisier in September 1774 describing his discovery of the previously unknown substance but Lavoisier never acknowledged receiving it.

The New Chemistry

Lavoisier was quite happy to accept Priestley's correction of some of the experimental errors he had made in his researches, since they helped him to solve some of the inconsistencies he had created in developing his new theories. He was soon working night and day testing the new gas in a series of careful and methodical experiments.

He became convinced that what Priestley had discovered was not in fact a different type of air but really just a component part of atmospheric air. In the famous 12-day experiment he performed in April 1776 he demonstrated that air,

29. Lavoisier conducts an experiment for visitors on human respiration with his wife recording

contrary to Priestley's belief, was actually made up of two or more different gases. From further experiments he was able to isolate oxygen, nitrogen and carbon dioxide from atmospheric air, and by careful calculation proved that oxygen made up one fifth of it. Furthermore, very importantly, he showed that it was in fact oxygen which is removed from the air when things are burnt. These discoveries laid the foundation of Lavoisier's new theory of combustion that when substances are burnt in air they combine with oxygen from the air to form an oxide. Thus combustion was not after all the release of so-called phlogiston, but the process of oxidation. He recognised, moreover, that respiration in living things and the rusting of iron, along with burning, were all forms of the same type of reaction.

These were findings of great importance for the scientific world. The phlogiston theory had suffered what proved to be a fatal defeat. In 1777/8 Lavoisier presented his paper – *Memoir on Combustion in General* – setting out his theory to the French *Académie*. It was in this paper that he introduced for the first time the new term *oxygen* to describe Priestley's *dephlogisticated air*.

Two Sides at War

Lavoisier's announcements to the French *Académie* were followed up by further work which later came to be called the *New Chemistry*, and which threw the scientific world into conflict. Fundamentally, the issue at stake was the overthrow of the phlogiston theory. Two opposing camps quickly developed – in Britain around Priestley and in France around Lavoisier.

Many scientists did in fact welcome Lavoisier's new theory. They had been frustrated with the phlogiston theory since it did not explain some of their own findings and they found it difficult to accept ideas like negative mass. Consequently Lavoisier's explanation soon became accepted by the majority of scientists. There was one notable exception – members of the celebrated Birmingham Lunar Society. Partly, perhaps, in misguided loyalty to their famous member, they rallied to Priestley's support and, at least in the early stages, most members remained firmly at the time in the phlogiston camp in the fight against the new French chemistry. A veritable war of words broke out. Accusations about Lavoisier's *"deceptions"* re-surfaced and he was branded as the *"arch-magician"*. Some phlogistonists even saw deceit in the way that the French scientist incorrectly spelt some English names.

Priestley himself fought stubbornly to defend the old theory. When a colleague tried to reconcile the two camps he was told firmly by Priestley that: "*I thank you for your ingenious and well-intended attempt to promote a peace between the two belligerent powers in chemistry; but I fear that your labour will be in vain. In my opinion, there can be no compromise*". He later complained of his treatment by the anti-phlogistonists as "*neither friendly nor agreeable to the rules of honourable war*".[14]

30. Priestley and Lavoisier, church minister and aristocrat

The bitterness felt on both sides ran deep and their dispute raged on well into the 1780s. A further cause of aggravation came in 1787 when Lavoisier and his scientific collaborators pressed ahead to recast the very language of chemistry in their publication, *Méthode de Nomenclature Chimique*. Up to that time, chemistry had suffered from the inadequacy of its technical language with *"a riot of names that hearkened back to the alchemists"* and even *"metals were named after pagan gods"*.[15] The revised terminology that Lavoisier and his colleagues finally produced in the *Nomenclature* heralded a much needed reform. It listed 700 chemicals with their old names translated into new ones and is still in use today. In the nineteenth century the French chemist, Adolphe Wurtz, had no doubt in claiming that *"La Chemie est une science française, elle fut constituée par Lavoisier"*.[16]

Nonetheless, the work was condemned by the die-hard phlogistonists as yet another attempt to undermine established traditions, and nothing less than *"a high treason against our ancestors"*.[17] Priestley took the opportunity to voice his opposition by condemning the changes not just on scientific grounds but as an exercise in French elitism. He prided himself on his efforts to present science in as democratic and clear way as possible so that general understanding could be maximised. He argued that the *New Chemistry* and the *Nomenclature*, in particular, were too exclusive and obscure, and thus would frustrate open and free debate.

However, by the end of the eighteenth century the battle was effectively over. Virtually all eminent scientists, including those in the Lunar Society, had become converts to the *New Chemistry*. The exception was Priestley who to his dying day resolutely defended the phlogiston theory. In 1800 he wrote to his friend Theophilus Lindsey, *"I have well considered all that my opponents have advanced and feel perfectly confident of the ground I stand upon ... Though nearly alone I am under no apprehension of defeat"*.[18] In the same year, he published from America his brochure entitled *The Doctrine of Phlogiston Upheld* in one last act of defiance; but by then his eminent adversary was no longer alive to read it.

The question that has to be asked is why did Priestley cling to the phlogiston theory when virtually all other reputable scientists came to reject it? True, there were a few imperfections in Lavoisier's work that were puzzling and were only cleared up later by other scientists. Perhaps in his isolation in America, Priestley had become resentful of being out of touch with modern scientific thought and he was unable to forgive the Frenchman for not acknowledging his work. However, the answer to Priestley's opposition probably comes back to his deep religious and theological convictions that his scientific investigations were contributing to the greater understanding of God's work on earth. Each of his great discoveries seem to have fortified his sense of awe and wonder. The concept of phlogiston with its spiritual, mysterious nature found a natural place in his thinking.

The Death of Lavoisier

The years before the French Revolution had been good ones for Lavoisier. He was an international celebrity, happily married, rich and powerful. At the height of his intellectual powers, he continued to contribute a stream of important scientific papers to the French *Académie*. However, soon after the Revolution broke out he began to be attacked by Marat and other radical journalists for his membership of the hated *Ferme Générale*. In 1793, the Reign of Terror broke out. The radical extremists, the Jacobins, had seized power and formed the dreaded Committee of Public Safety headed by Robespierre.

Before long the tumbrels carrying bound victims to the guillotine were rolling through the streets of Paris. Urged on by the mob to *"bring the bloodsuckers to justice"*, the Committee turned its attention to the former *tax farmers*. Lavoisier knew he was in great danger. His scientific collaborators deserted him, and his friends no longer gathered together at his dinner table. As the witch hunt against the *tax farmers* intensified, his laboratory was closed and his papers seized. At the end of 1793 he was imprisoned along with the other *farmers*. In a trial that lasted less than four hours, Lavoisier and 27 other *farmers* were convicted and sentenced to execution. When Lavoisier pleaded for time to complete some scientific work, it is said that the Judge replied, *"This Republic had no need of scientists; let justice take its course"*.[19] Lavoisier died with great dignity and composure. In a last letter to his cousin he wrote:

> *I have had a fairly long life, above all a very happy one, and I think that I shall be remembered with some regrets and perhaps leave some reputation behind me. What more could I ask? The events in which I am involved will probably save me from the troubles of old age. I shall die in full possession of my faculties.*[20]

He was executed on 8 May 1794. It took the French government just one and a half years to exonerate him. When his belongings were returned to his widow, a brief note was attached reading *"to the widow of Lavoisier who was falsely executed"*.[21]

It is a sad commentary on the antipathy that had developed between the two scientists that, after Lavoisier was guillotined, Priestley does not seem to have offered any condolences to his French friends. For Lavoisier's part, as time went by he had become more and more contemptuous of the phlogistonists like Priestley as backward looking and little more than charlatans. He did at least draft a letter to Priestley following the Birmingham riots to express his and fellow scientists' regret to a man who had *"opened up new paths in science"*, but there is no evidence of Priestley ever receiving such a letter.[22]

After Lavoisier's death, his wife Marie-Anne was determined that his position and reputation in the scientific world should never be forgotten. She ran a salon and hosted parties for many eminent scientists where they could discuss the New Chemistry and other ideas. She privately published Lavoisier's unfinished memoirs and circulated them to her friends. In 1805 she married an American, Benjamin Thompson but they separated within four years. Marie-Anne died at the age of 78.

Conclusion

For all their differences and animosity, the lives of Priestley and Lavoisier had much in common. Both were intellectuals who loved their countries and worked to improve the lot of mankind. Both incurred enemies and suffered badly at the hands of their countrymen. Priestley was driven from his country to exile in America, while France sent Lavoisier to the guillotine. Both were great scientists who in different circumstances might have collaborated as a near perfect team for their talents and skills were complementary – Priestley, the peerless experimenter, and Lavoisier, the brilliant theorist.

Although to Priestley and Scheele must go the credit for actually discovering oxygen, neither grasped its full significance, and it was Lavoisier who recognised its true nature and explained the vital role it played in combustion. The Frenchman was able to throw off the shackles of the past in a way that Priestley could not, and to bring his findings into the framework of a unified theory as did other great scientists such as Copernicus, Newton, Darwin and Einstein. We can criticise Lavoisier for unethical scientific conduct but no one can now challenge his importance to modern chemistry. Lavoisier's tragedy was to live during the course of another momentous revolution that was blind to his greatness.

CHAPTER 8

Bishop Samuel Horsley
(1733–1806)
The Grand Mufti

The attack made by Bishop Samuel Horsley on Joseph Priestley's religious writings during the 1780s created one of the fiercest controversies of the age. Although he is little known today, Horsley deserves more recognition. He was rightly regarded as the *"ablest ecclesiastical statesman of the late eighteenth century and also the most effective"*.[1] An exceptional Church leader and reforming bishop, he made a vigorous and stout defence of the Anglican Church, and its virtue, at a crucial stage in its development.

In appearance the two contestants were a world apart – the bull-like, rotund, high church conservative in one corner, and the spare, frugal and liberal Dissenter in the other. They had opposite and deeply held religious and political beliefs. Whereas Priestley relished the spirit of the age, welcoming revolution and change, Horsley was a staunch conservative in religious, social and political matters. He maintained that, once established, governments received a divine legitimacy which placed an obligation on the citizen's allegiance and submission. His assertion that the people of the country *"had nothing to do with*

31. Bishop Samuel Horsley

laws but to obey them", saw him satirised as the Turkish autocrat – the Grand Mufti.

And yet their lives had some remarkable similarities. They were born in the same year, 1733, and Horsley outlived Priestley by only two years. They had intellectual interests in common, and both were enthusiastic Greek and mathematical scholars. Horsley's early career too was spent as a scientist and he kept his scientific instruments until the end of his life. Like Priestley, he was a Fellow of the Royal Society, and both shared a particular interest in the voyages of overseas exploration. They passionately defended their differences, but they took a common stand on some of the great moral issues of the day such as the slave trade. They both argued for complete toleration for English Catholics. And however outspoken and pugnacious they were in their public lives, in private they each showed a warm and deeply sensitive side to their character.

Early Life
Samuel Horsley was the son of the Rev. John Horsley, a lecturer at St Martin-in-the-Fields, and his wife, Anne Hamilton. Samuel went to Trinity Hall, Cambridge as a law student in 1751 and was admitted to the Middle Temple in 1755. Although never called to the Bar, he gained some useful experience in preparing and presenting cases which stood him in good stead later in life. He decided to abandon a legal career and to follow his father into the Church of England. He became a parish priest in 1758 but was soon drawn to intellectual rather than pastoral interests, and was elected to the Fellowship of the Royal Society in 1767. It was the Society that formed the focus of his life over the next decade.

Ambitious, he took his duties very seriously and was determined to raise the Society's standards. By 1771 he had become a member of the Council and in 1773 he was appointed as one of the two Secretaries of the Society. Two years later, he proposed to the Council that he should publish and edit the complete edition of all the works of Sir Isaac Newton This was a massive and bold undertaking for the mass of papers left by Newton was extremely daunting. One account, probably apocryphal, alleged that Horsley, when asked to inspect a box of Newton's manuscripts and papers totalling some 1.2 million words with a view to publication, recoiled in horror and slammed the lid tight![2] In fact, he tackled the task with great determination and made good progress, especially at a time of some personal unhappiness since his young wife, Mary, died in 1777, leaving him with two small children to bring up. His edition of Newton's work, which appeared in five volumes during 1779–85, was a considerable achievement. It established Horsley's reputation as a serious Newtonian scholar.

Nonetheless, there was some criticism made that he had given inadequate attention to Newton's religious writings and had even destroyed some religious papers which purported to show Newton to be a Unitarian by faith. It has to be said that given Horsley's High Church views and, contrary to Newton, his firm belief in the Trinity, Horsley does seem to have been a curious choice for the Newtonian project. Although there is simply no hard evidence that he actually destroyed any of Newton's papers, latest research seems to confirm that he shied away from publishing any evidence of Newton's interest in alchemy and his religious beliefs.[3]

Horsley's time at the Society came to an abrupt end in 1779 when he resigned the Secretaryship and lost his place on the Council. We cannot be certain what precipitated the events. Horsley may well have decided to step down, reckoning that his chances of further advancement were weakened by the changes in the Society's presidency at that time. The new president, the 35 year old Joseph Banks, was ten years younger than Horsley and his interests in natural history were very different from the Society's traditional disciplines of astronomy and mathematics to which Horsley himself was strongly committed. On the other hand, the chances are that he was simply ousted by internal politics; if so he was not a man to forgive and forget. When a few years later trouble broke out at the Society, Horsley was determined to use it to settle some old scores.

Joseph Banks, as President, kept a tight personal control over the business of the Society which irked some members. Matters came to a head in 1783 when, under pressure from Banks, the Council forced the resignation of the mathematician Dr Charles Hutton from the office of the Society's Secretary

32. Joseph Banks, President of the Royal Society. His commitment to natural history led to Gillray caricaturing him as "the great South Sea caterpillar"

for Foreign Affairs. Hutton appealed to the Society at large, and his friends, including Horsley, organised two successive meetings thanking him for his services and exonerating him from the charges made of inefficiency. Horsley lost no time in channelling the agitation into a general attack on *"the entire administration of the Royal Society under Banks' presidency, alleging infringement of chartered rights, interference with freedom of elections, and mismanagement of the Committee of Papers"*.[4] He threatened that he knew enough wrongs to keep the Society in debate for the whole winter, and perhaps beyond the winter. The venom and vindictiveness with which the attack was conducted brought the business of the Society to a standstill. It seems that Horsley was determined to show up Banks and perhaps even replace him as president. In the event however the dissidents were defeated and Banks won a vote of confidence. Whereupon Horsley succeeded in further alienating Society members by publishing anonymously an exposé of the dissensions and debates of the Society. By 1784 his support had melted away and his career as a scientist and academician was effectively over.

The events left Horsley bitter and disappointed but he had shown his mettle as a formidable protagonist and someone certainly not averse to public controversy. His ability was recognised by the Bishop of London who as early as 1781 had appointed him as his chaplain and made him Archdeacon of St Albans. As a High Church Tory, Horsley was soon busy in the defence of the traditions and status of both Church and King, and publicly criticised what he saw were the excesses of the Enlightenment.

Horsley was convinced that the Church of England was the most important bulwark against the rise of atheism and republicanism. In his opinion it was the Dissenters who posed the greatest threat. And no one more so than the leader of the Unitarians, Joseph Priestley, publicly ridiculed by Horsley as one of those *"predestinarians versed in Physics"*.[5] His antipathy towards the Dissenters never wavered; when he was later made the Bishop of St David's, he wanted his churchmen to extend hospitality to French Catholic clergy on the grounds that he had more in common with them than with Dissenters.

It was the Dissenters' campaign to get the Test and Corporation Acts repealed during the 1780s that was at the heart of the conflict between Priestley and Horsley. Horsley was determined that this should not happen, and the zeal and energy with which he successfully orchestrated the opposition soon established his position as a very influential member of the High Church party. The scene was set for the fiercest religious confrontation of the age, the Trinitarian controversy between Bishop Horsley and Joseph Priestley.

Controversy

The actual conflict with Horsley was triggered by Priestley's publication in 1782, entitled the *History of the Corruptions of Christianity*. Priestley was bent on answering those in leading scientific and fashionable circles who openly expressed their disbelief in Christianity, and not least those who had offended him during his visit to Paris in 1774 with his patron Lord Shelburne (Chapter 7). He also had one particularly important *"unbeliever"* firmly in his sights, the historian Edward Gibbon, who in 1776 had produced his classic work on the *Decline and Fall of the Roman Empire* in which he had expressed his deep scepticism of early Christianity.

Priestley's *History* in essence formed a direct attack by him on the essential doctrines of the Church of England that had survived the Reformation. He sought to demonstrate that true Christianity embodied the beliefs of the early church, and that all the departures from the true faith that had accumulated over the centuries were corruptions introduced simply to satisfy prevailing conditions and opinions. Priestley's book impressed many liberals in Britain and America (especially Thomas Jefferson (Chapter 12)) but infuriated the orthodox.

Unsurprisingly, it was Priestley's views on the Trinity that caused the greatest storm. This to Priestley was the most important of all the corruptions. He argued that the faith of the earliest Christians was in fact Unitarian, and that it had been Christian thinkers of the second and third centuries who, under Platonic influences, had attributed a separate divinity to Christ. It was, he maintained, only at the Council of Nicea in AD 325 that the supremacy of the Father over the Son was abandoned and the full Trinitarian doctrine adopted by the orthodox churches. In his conclusion, Priestley threw down a two fold challenge. First, he called upon unbelievers, and notably Gibbon, to defend their opinions publicly with him; and secondly he exhorted the bishops of the established church to relax their attitude towards those clergymen, who, like Priestley's friend Theophilus Lindsey, felt they could no longer subscribe fully to the Thirty-Nine Articles of the Church of England.

Gibbon, none too politely, refused to be drawn into a dispute, calling Priestley an even greater unbeliever than himself. Priestley's book in fact caused a storm of protest. It was banned in parts of England and even publicly burned in Holland. However, Priestley's challenge was not one that the Established Church could afford to disregard. It was a Church badly in need of defence and reassurance; it could not ignore the evangelical challenge from the Methodist Revival, nor the deep economic, social and intellectual changes taking place throughout the country, all of which had left many in the clergy anxious and in a low state of morale. Besides Lindsey, a few other unorthodox clergy had resigned their livings after Parliament had rejected the Feathers' Tavern petition (Chapter 6). Undoubtedly too there were many in the clergy who were lazy and held in contempt. The difficulty was that too many Anglican bishops were complacent about the state of affairs and content to lead an easy life at a time when strong leadership was required. It was left to Archdeacon Horsley to respond and he eagerly rose to the challenge.

In May 1783, he used a lengthy visitation address to the clergy of the Archdeaconry of St Albans to defend the Church and to warn the clergy against Priestley's work. So began the famous controversy between the two men which extended over a period of seven years.

Horsley had worked hard to build up his knowledge of the early Christian historical texts so that he could respond as effectively as possible to Priestley. Although he did not wish to avoid answering the central argument about the alleged "corruptions" and Priestley's attack on the truth of the Trinity, he also was very much aware of the pressing need to undermine his opponent's scholastic reputation and accuracy in religious matters in the eyes of the Anglican clergy. He concentrated therefore on pointing out inaccuracies in translations that Priestley had made and the latter's misunderstanding of Platonism. Writing later in the Preface to his collective tracts, he declared that *"it seems that the most effectual preservation against the intended mischief, would be to destroy the writer's credit and the authority of his name"*.[6]

Priestley, on the other hand, privately thought that Horsley's response was arrogant and betrayed weaknesses in the Bishop's own understanding and scholarship. He maintained there were eleven serious historical points which his opponent had not answered. He tried in vain to draw Horsley into a full public debate on the main question of the doctrine of the Trinity, but met with a blank refusal on the grounds that: *"it was not at all my intention to open a regular controversy with you upon the subject ... My attack ... was not so much upon the opinions that you maintain, however I may hold them in abhorrence, as upon the credit of your Narrative"*.[7]

Priestley however persisted with his arguments, and each time Horsley was forced to make at least some response to the points raised. As the controversy dragged on over the years, both protagonists showed considerable ingenuity and scholarship in addressing their differences, especially Priestley's central argument that there had been a significant change in the doctrines of the church from apostolic times until the Council of Nicea. Both men, too, appreciated the importance of the publicity which arose from the controversy, not only to justify their cause, but to cast aspersions on one another's character. Horsley scathingly referred to Priestley's *"lucky"* scientific discoveries, and disparaged him as *"this emeritus professor of Greek in the late academy at Warrington"*.[8] In return, Priestley felt confident enough to dismiss his opponent by appealing *"to all the learned world whether any man pretending in scholarship ever undertook the study of a question of literature less prepared for it or acquitted himself so wretchedly in it"*.[9]

It was a habit of Priestley to use challenging remarks as a method of discovering truth, but as shown in other contexts, these too often could be turned against him by his enemies to damaging effect. In the middle of the controversy with Horsley, Priestley recklessly used Guy Fawkes Day in 1785 to make his outspoken sermon during which he referred to *"laying gunpowder, grain by grain, under the old building of error and superstition"* (Chapter 1). The inflammatory nature of such a statement was a gift to Horsley, who thereafter took care to make extracts available from Priestley's writings to show that he was not only a religious extremist but a man with subversive opinions dangerous to the State. He personally encouraged the Birmingham Anglican magistrates where Priestley was resident to be prepared to nip *"Dr Priestley's goodly projects in the bud; which nothing would be so likely to ripen to a dangerous effect"*.[10]

By 1789 Horsley considered that he had won the arguments. He effectively withdrew from the controversy though not before republishing his earlier contributions in a single volume. Not surprisingly, however, opinion differed sharply as to who had the best of the controversy. Contemporary supporters of the Church predictably argued that Horsley had showed superior learning and ability, and Priestley was guilty of mistranslating and sophistry. Horsley's grandson, Heneage Horsley Jebb, in a careful but uncritical biography, concluded that Horsley had *"completely vanquished Priestley"*.[11]

However, by declining to comment in depth on Priestley's important work on the Early Opinions concerning Jesus Christ and the Trinity, Horsley left himself open to the charge that he had become more intent with the controversy than the truth. For the Unitarians, writers like Thomas Belsham in the early nineteenth century redressed the balance by pointing to several important points that Horsley failed to address during their debates, and declared that Priestley's victory was *"decisive and complete"*. In recent times Horsley's biographer F.C. Mather concluded that Priestley was correct in claiming *"that an important change in the Church's teaching regarding the person of Christ and the Trinity took place in the second and third centuries AD under Platonic influences though not in portraying it as a corruption"*.[12]

To sum up, it was a conflict from which in fact both men could take some satisfaction. Horsley without doubt had showed considerable erudition, energy and skill during the controversy and he emerged from it with a much enhanced national reputation. And as far as the Church of England was concerned, he had achieved his purpose of restoring a measure of confidence among the clergy and few left the Church to become Unitarians. Horsley was suitably rewarded with a prebendary (an honorary post) at Gloucester Cathedral, and in 1788 he was promoted to the See of St David's. As for Priestley, he and his supporters were convinced that his arguments had been superior and that he had vindicated the Unitarian position. His doughty defence of the Utilitarian belief gained him much respect and prestige among the Rational Dissenters and it confirmed his place as their acknowledged leader. Perhaps, therefore, Belsham has come close to the mark when he concluded that both of the original contestants had retired content, Priestley with his victory and Horsley with his mitre.

A Reforming Bishop

Having established his reputation within the Church, in his subsequent career Horsley showed himself to be an energetic and reforming bishop. Many came to regard him as the most effective bishop on the bench. He worked hard to better the position of the clergy but was prepared to attack the abuses of his time and he took a particularly tough line on the scandal of the absence or non-residence of a considerable part of the parochical clergy from their parishes.

He was convinced of the importance of practical Christianity and a genuine interest in helping the poor. He believed firmly in the importance of improving the understanding of Christian dogma among the uneducated classes and this led him to support the Charity Schools. On then other hand, as with many high Anglicans of the time, he was not happy with the Sunday schools; they were largely cross-denominational and Horsley feared that they were channels for malign religious and political teaching. In recognition of his services, William Pitt the Younger later appointed him Bishop of Rochester in 1793 and then of St Asaph in 1802. However, the very highest positions in the Church eluded him.

The French Revolution

During his later years Horsley sided even more firmly with the ruling class. He was convinced that the stability of the social, legal and constitutional dimensions of Britain, and the happiness of its people, depended heavily on order and restraint. In his opinion, any violent and factious attack on an established government had to be seen as a rebellion against God.

Not surprisingly therefore, he greeted the French Revolution as a cataclysmic event for mankind on which there could be no compromise. To his mind, it threatened the very preservation of Christian society within Europe, and Britain was the only country that could mount an effective resistance. He expressed his views openly whenever possible but it was the occasion of his State Sermon at Westminster Abbey to the House of Lords on 30 January 1793 which provided just the national platform he was looking for.

The Sermon marked the Anniversary of the Martyrdom of Charles I and its timing could not have been more propitious for Horsley. Just over a week earlier Louis XVI had been executed in Paris. The fear of Jacobinism and revolution in Britain had thrown the government and propertied class into a state of high anxiety, a fear intensified by religious prophecies that the coming millennium would herald a major transformation of society. It was a time for leadership and reassurance.

Horsley did not disappoint his audience. In a typically clear and forceful sermon, he exposed the follies of revolution and reaffirmed the divine legitimacy of government. The sermon began moderately enough. His High Church views, he said, did not entail that any single view of government was especially sanctioned by Providence. Monarchies for example had no greater sanctity than any other form of established governments. But the forms of government that existed at that time were the work of human policy under the control of God's general over-ruling guidance. Thus in Britain, he agreed that the King through constitutional arrangements, such as Magna Carta, the Bill of Rights and the Act of Settlement, had entered into an *"explicit, patent, and precise"* legal contract with the nation; since this had divine legitimacy the people had no danger to fear from a Whig sovereign. But equally it was not law or Acts of Parliament that obliged people to obey governments but the obligation derived primarily from the will of God *"that first principle of religious duty which requires that man conform himself . . . with the will and purpose of his Maker"*.[13]

His forceful anti-revolutionary oratory had his audience in thrall; during his peroration the entire congregation rose to its feet and remained standing, deeply moved to the end. In highly emotional terms Horsley concluded by outlining the blessings of the British constitution, its religion, liberty and the majesty of its sovereign, and contrasted them with the execution of Louis XVI. He exclaimed, *"This foul murder, and these barbarities, has filled the measure of the guilt and infamy of France. O my country read the horror of thy own deed in this recent heightened imitation!"*.[14]

As the war with France dragged on, Horsley's fear of imminent invasion became almost paranoid and he demanded that the clergy itself should form an armed militia as the final defence. Other churchmen, alarmed by Horsley's reaction, urged bishops to *"check the arming influenza of their inferior brethren"*.[15] But there was no holding Horsley back. He insisted that he was ready to *"level the musket and to trail the pike"*, and at St Asaph he helped to mobilise the local militia, even encouraging it to exercise and to drill on the palace lawn.[16]

He continued to oppose vehemently any attempts to establish peace with France. He remained convinced that the apocalyptic prophecies surrounding the coming millennium were being truly borne out and that the Revolution and the rise of Napoleon Bonaparte, the Anti-Christ, confirmed the existence of a grand international conspiracy against Christian civilisation in general. He claimed that without doubt the world was facing its greatest threat since *"the moment of our Lord's departure from the earth"*.[17]

Bishop Horsley's final years were not happy ones. His second wife, Sarah, who suffered from poor health died in 1805. His son, Heneage, disgraced his father by getting into bad debts and fled to Scotland to avoid arrest. Samuel Horsley died in Brighton on 4 October 1806. At his death he was insolvent having failed to renew a life insurance policy, and his effects, including a fine library, were sold off to pay his debts.

Conclusion

When Priestley left for America in 1794, Horsley felt able to exult that the patriarch of the sect had fled and at last the *"orators and oracles of Birmingham and Essex Street are dumb"*.[18] The two men never really understood one another. Each was convinced of his own righteousness, and prepared to fight tenaciously in public for their opinions. It seemed inevitable that these two champions of conservatism and radicalism were destined at some time to lock horns with one another. It is easy to caricature Horsley as an over-indulgent, pig-headed reactionary. But in truth, Priestley came up against a man who could match him in erudition, conviction and in ability, and who was truly a formidable adversary.

The animosity of their controversy, and its extravagant language, should not disguise its significance. Both Horsley and Priestley emerged from it with their reputation and authority among their supporters much enhanced. Anglicans and Dissenters, each on their own terms, drew strength and reassurance from the performance of the respective protagonists. The controversy demonstrated the exceptional abilities of two men at the peak of their powers. Impressively, both displayed considerable independence of thought and moral courage in the way they resolutely held to their beliefs and defended the doctrines of their respective Churches.

CHAPTER 9

Thomas Cooper
(1759–1839)
The Resolute Firebrand

Thomas Jefferson, third President of America, once called Thomas Cooper *"the greatest man in America in the powers of mind, and in acquired information"*.[1] President John Adams, the second President, regarded him somewhat less favourably as a *"learned, ingenious, scientific, and talented madcap"*.[2] Thomas Cooper enjoyed life to the full; he had wide intellectual interests and a remarkably varied if tempestuous career. He was a prolific writer and political activist throughout his life, and a sometime manufacturer, lawyer, physician

33. Thomas Cooper

and science professor. Often controversial, he was prepared to go to jail for his outspoken views. He became an American citizen and made important contributions to the public life of the young American Republic.

Physically, Cooper was described as *"a man of low stature, but robust, well proportioned and very compactly built, his head was large and finely developed, and uncommonly round, his neck stout and thick, his chest capacious"*.[3] There was a winning simplicity and directness about him; he was trained as a lawyer and never used a word, illustration or argument that was not to the point.

Priestley was some 20 years older than Cooper and they first met when Priestley was around 50. Priestley was attracted by the energy and personality of the younger man and they quickly became friends. They had much in common in terms of their intellectual interests, ideas and temperament. They collaborated on scientific research and both were readily drawn into political controversy. They both felt compelled to leave England for America. Their close friendship was strained at times and not always in Priestley's best interests, but it was one that was to have important consequences for both their lives.

Early Life
Thomas Cooper was born in London in 1759, the son of a wealthy land owner. He studied classics at Oxford University until 1779 but did not take a degree because, it is said, he refused to recite the Creed and to sign the Thirty-Nine Articles of the Church of England. In the same year, he married Alice Greenwood who had inherited a considerable fortune from her father. They had five children, all of whom later came to America with them. After studying medicine for a short time in London, Cooper and his wife moved to Manchester in 1780, the same year that Joseph Priestley went to Birmingham after his leaving his post with Lord Shelburne. Once settled in Manchester, Cooper followed his interests in medicine, philosophy and law. He was a barrister in Lancaster from 1787 to 1790 and became an enthusiastic member of the prestigious Manchester Literary and Philosophical Society.

At that time, Manchester was the commercial centre of the fast growing cotton trade and Cooper soon became involved in the associated bleaching and dyeing industry. Very likely, it was his interest in the chemistry of this industry that first brought him into contact with Joseph Priestley in the early 1780s. Before long, Cooper was spending many hours in Priestley's excellent laboratory in Birmingham where the two men conducted together experiments of value to the chemical developments of the Industrial Revolution.

Cooper was enthusiastic about the need for political reform in Britain and his relationship with Priestley would soon have alerted him to contemporary political issues. Always a very industrious man, he began to make many and diverse radical contributions to various political publications, especially those of the Manchester Literary and Philosophical Society. In 1787, he published his

Propositions respecting the Foundation of Civil Government which set out forcefully his personal philosophical and political views. He believed unequivocally in the sovereignty of the people, and the right of popular resistance to oppression. His views drew heavily on the ideas of Locke, but it is clear that the inspiration for his political philosophy owed much to the influence of Priestley. Cooper later attributed Priestley's essay in 1768 on the *First Principles of Civil Government* as being the first plain, popular and brief book on the principles of civil government.[4]

In Manchester, Cooper became a very active reformer. He organised petitions and promoted committees. He attacked the slave trade, drawing his fellow citizens' attention to what he condemned as that *"infamous and impolitic traffic"*. Soon, he was working hard with Priestley and others to repeal the century old Test and Corporation Acts (Chapter 6). By early in 1790 he had become identified with a particularly radical group of Protestant Dissenters in Manchester and was suspected by the authorities of having more sinister and far-reaching designs than just the repeal of the Acts. Cooper certainly wanted to see the back of the Acts, but did not disguise the fact that he considered the repeal of other penal laws of greater importance. His reputation amongst the governing class as a dangerous revolutionary grew and from now on Cooper was a marked man and his activities were watched closely.

Living Dangerously

Joseph Priestley, on the other hand, had no doubts about the virtues of his young friend. He appreciated the help he had provided in organising opposition to the Test and Corporation Acts, and he regarded him as an excellent chemist. In December 1789, Priestley and other distinguished scientists nominated Cooper to become a Fellow of the Royal Society as a *"Gentleman well versed in Natural Philosophy and particularly in Chemistry"*. The ballot took place in the following March but the nomination was defeated by 24 votes to 20. Priestley was indignant that his friend had been rejected. He wrote bitterly to the President, Sir Joseph Banks, complaining that many church dignitaries and the King's librarians had voted against Cooper simply *"from principles which would equally lead to my own exclusion from the Society"*.[5] He organised a second nomination in May 1791, this time backed by an even stronger array of scientists such as Josiah Wedgwood and Matthew Boulton. Again the nomination was rejected. Priestley was now convinced that the rejection of a man, whose knowledge of chemistry and philosophy he claimed *"far exceeded his own"*, was indeed entirely attributable to the opposition of vested ecclesiastical and political interests. The failure to get Cooper elected added significantly to Priestley's growing disillusionment with the Society. Although he did not formally resign, he records in his memoirs that he *"at length withdrew myself from them"* and he ceased to send his papers to the Society.[6]

Little is known about how Cooper himself felt about the rejection but there was certainly no slackening in his business and political interests. The French Revolution was greeted enthusiastically by him and other political reformers throughout the land, and Cooper was amongst the leading activists in both London and Manchester. In 1790 he and a radical friend, Thomas Walker, became the leaders of the newly formed Manchester Constitutional Party. These Societies had been formed across the country to oppose the conservative activities of bodies like the Church and King Clubs which had became increasingly alarmed at the *"wild fears and seditious doctrines"* of the reformers. Edmund Burke, the conservative politician, played a prominent part in publicly denouncing reformers like Cooper as linked to the French Jacobins and a threat to civilised society and its institutions (Chapter 10).

Tensions between the two sides continued to run high especially as events in France took an ugly and menacing turn, but Cooper was one of a group of reformers who resolutely spurned advice to moderate their activity. Despite threats of violence, the radical Constitutional Societies decided to hold a series of dinners on 14 July 1791 to celebrate the second anniversary of the French Revolution. Although no violence occurred in Manchester, at the Society dinner attended by Cooper in Birmingham it was very different. A mob was urged on by the King and Church party to attack the homes of well-known Dissenters and Society members. This was the outrage that had disastrous results for the Priestley family, and led to their flight to London.

Cooper was shocked by the Birmingham riots and resigned from the Manchester Literary and Philosophical Society when it failed to express its sympathy to Priestley. But he remained active politically and, in 1792, he decided to travel to France with the son of James Watt to see at first hand what was happening there. In Paris, they were received warmly. They lost no time in addressing various societies, including the Jacobin Club, expressing their support for the French constitution. The title of *Citizen of France* was conferred on Cooper, and without too much thought he and Watt agreed to take part in a revolutionary parade and to display the British flag. Predictably, this provoked an immediate outcry in Britain and their action was fiercely denounced by Burke during a debate in the House of Commons on the subject of reform. Cooper was forced to return to England to answer the criticism. He did his best to assuage his critics by issuing his pamphlet *Reply to Burke's Invective*, in which he declared that democratic reform was his intention, not the overthrow of British institutions, but few were impressed.

The French *Reign of Terror* gathered pace in the early summer of 1792 arousing fears of war and invasion in Britain. The Government decided that the time had come to curb the activities of the reformers (Chapter 10). In May 1792 a royal proclamation was issued against all *"wicked and seditious writings"*. Cooper characteristically reacted by protesting against the proclamation and continued to publish articles on the French Revolution and the evils of war in the *The Manchester Herald* which by now he was editing. In December 1792, the government issued a second proclamation against sedition. Cooper and Walker were singled out personally as "*seditious individuals*" by the Manchester Church and King Association and it urged magistrates to demand that the two men swear an oath of allegiance to George III.

When, in 1793, war with France finally broke out, the sedition proclamations were fully implemented. *The Herald* was closed down. Rumours abounded that both Cooper and Walker were to be charged with high treason and they faced the real prospect of imprisonment and possible deportation to Australia. At the same time Cooper's business foundered; the war had triggered an economic depression and Cooper's bleaching business collapsed and he became bankrupt. Despite pleas from some of his friends to stay in England, Cooper decided that his best course of action was to start a new life in America.

America
For some time Cooper had become friendly with the Priestley's eldest son, Joseph, who had also resolved to leave England as his own prospects had been badly damaged by the attacks on his father. Both he and Cooper, together with Priestley's third son, Henry, set sail for America in August 1793 with the declared objective of finding a location in America which would provide a haven for British Dissenters and other like minded people. They soon identified the region of the Susquehanna River in central Pennsylvania as a likely looking place, and decided that the small town of Northumberland would make a suitable centre for the scheme.

Prior to completing the emigration process, Cooper briefly returned to England in February 1794 to collect the rest of his family. By this time, his friend Walker and others were under trial at Lancaster Assizes for sedition. Some accounts suggest that Cooper tried to help with the defence of his former associates but, under fear of arrest himself, he seems generally to have kept a low profile. He did however during this time publish his work *Some Information Respecting America* which painted a very positive picture of America for would-be emigrants, and of the proposed settlement on the Susquehanna in particular.

In April 1794, Priestley and his wife embarked for America. Since Cooper had been close to them throughout their plans for their departure, it is fair to assume that his enthusiastic description about America, and the Land Scheme, had a major bearing on their final decision to leave England and indeed on where to settle in the new Republic. Priestley would certainly have taken careful note of Cooper's prediction of the bright future for learning in America and the likelihood of "*the total absence of anxiety respecting the future success of a*

34. An early view of Northumberland on the Susquehanna River

family".[7] Although Cooper did not himself accompany the Priestleys on their voyage, he left Britain later in the same year.

Life in America
Soon after Priestley's arrival in America, and much to his great disappointment, it was apparent that the proposed Land Scheme on the Susquehanna was not going to succeed. Few immigrants were prepared to buy land in the area and settle there, and the Scheme was officially abandoned in March 1795 after a particularly harsh winter. Priestley was now over 60 and the news hit him hard. He wrote to a former friend, President Adams, that, "*tho that scheme has failed, I cannot remove any more*".[8] Priestley remained in touch with Cooper, and despite their disappointment, both decided to settle with their families in the vicinity of the failed scheme in Northumberland.

These proved to be arduous times for both families, and Priestley admitted that the climate and manner of living were very different from those in England. He found the remoteness of the location and its poor communications hard to live with. Letters from England took four months to arrive. However, with his customary fortitude, Priestley with Mary's help soon set about building a new home big enough to house his family and scientific equipment, and characteristically laid plans for developing a college in the locality.

Cooper also struggled. He was impoverished and naively hoped to make a living by farming, a task for which he was singularly unfitted. He and his family lived in a makeshift two-roomed log cabin to which he added another room "*nailed to some Posts set in the grounds where I live*".[9] When the French traveller, Rochefoucauld, visited Northumberland around 1795 he painted an unfavourable picture of the lives of both men. He was not impressed with the austerity of the Priestley household and what he described as their cold and haughty manner. And as for Cooper, he remarked that, "*He is undoubtedly a man of parts, of a restless mind, ill adapted to find happiness in a retired rural life*".[10]

Priestley longed especially for the company of his English friends, but their visits were few and far between, and he and Cooper became depressed by their failure to attract other Englishmen to settle near them in Northumberland. Predictably, Priestley and his family felt that they had been deceived by the original proprietors of the Land Scheme, and not least by Cooper's part in it. His extravagant description of America and his enthusiasm for land speculation showed, said Priestley, his want "*of prudence and attention to small concerns*".[11] By 1795, relations between Priestley and Cooper had noticeably cooled.

But there was another problem causing friction between the two men – religion. Even before he left England, Priestley had been concerned about Cooper's growing religious unbelief, and by the fact that he had, moreover, got into the habit of "*profane swearing in conversation*".[12] Priestley had become increasingly troubled too that Cooper's religious disbelief might be having a baleful influence on his sons.

Cooper was certainly not a religious man in the conventional sense, but more a religious free-thinker. He was often outspoken, even aggressive, about his agnosticism. Fundamentally, he had no time for mystery and could not understand why others could what he termed "*loiter in the shadows*". As one of his biographers has asserted, "*The God he worshipped was Truth and his creed was Freedom*", and he was a man who "*turned the bright light of truth into every department of life*".[13] Probably out of his regard for Priestley, Cooper gave a nominal adherence to Unitarianism which seemed to him to offer the most rational and comprehensive theological belief. And when he was living in the community in Northumberland, it is likely that he would have at least attended the religious services which Priestley held there every Sunday. Nonetheless, Priestley readily admitted to his friends of his regret that they had such a great difference of opinion over religion.

Political Activity

By the end of 1795, Cooper had given up hope of making a living from farming and he turned to the law. The year before he had taken American citizenship, which Priestley never did, and he was soon admitted to the American Bar.

However, he earned little from his legal work. Priestley was well aware that his friend was struggling financially and did his best to help him. Priestley was clearly lonely after the death of his wife in 1796 and shortly afterwards Cooper came to live with Priestley in his new house. He helped Priestley set up the laboratory attached to Priestley's house and they once more conducted experiments together. It was there that Cooper successfully produced the newly discovered element, potassium.

In 1797, in an effort to help his friend find employment, Priestley took what proved to be a fateful step by asking President John Adams, who was in power at the time, to consider Cooper for a government post. It was to cost both Priestley and his friend dearly. The request was ignored with apparent disdain by Adams. Later on when news of the application somehow became public, it was eagerly seized upon by William Cobbett and Federalist writers to accuse the two *"emigrant philosophers"* of campaigning politically against Adams and his administration simply out of spite and revenge for the President's rejection of Cooper (Chapter 11).

In their early years in America, both Priestley and Cooper tried to heed the advice of their friends to keep clear of the feverish state of American party politics at that time (Chapter 12). However, neither had the temperament to remain silent for long about issues which meant a lot to them. True, both were sorely provoked by the vitriolic attacks on them by William Cobbett and others (Chapter 11), but they gradually allowed themselves to be drawn into political activities without too much thought of the likely repercussions, especially in the run up to the Presidential election of 1800. Both men sympathised with the anti-Federalists or Democratic Party led by Thomas Jefferson, and could not resist expressing their opinions publicly. It is likely that they encouraged one another, but Cooper was prepared to be the more active and aggressive of the two. Even Priestley thought him *"something too quick"*,[14] and Cooper may well have been the dominant partner in some of the more injudicious incidents into which the two men were drawn.

In 1799, Cooper had undertaken the editorship of the *Northumberland Gazette*. He wasted little time in personally composing many letters and articles which amounted to a very hostile attack on the ruling administration of President Adams, and made clear his support for Jefferson. Cooper collected all his newspaper articles into a book entitled *Essays on Political Arithmetic* (1799) in which he enumerated all that he believed to be the misconceived and illiberal measures of the Adams administration. He attacked the Sedition Act which it had enacted, and he made a strong plea for the freedom of the press.

The *Essays* certainly had the backing of Priestley and were widely distributed. Since they provided invaluable ammunition for the Democratic opponents of Adams, predictably the full wrath of the ruling party was now turned on the two men. Adams condemned Cooper *"as a rash man, and had led Dr Priestley into all his errors in England, and he feared would lead him into others in America*". He dismissed the attack on his administration as, "*a meaner, a more artful, or more malicious libel has not appeared*".[15] Adams also concurred with the allegation that the real reason for the onslaught on his government was the earlier failure of Cooper to secure a government job.

Undeterred, Cooper seems to have been determined to become a political martyr. He made an even more inflammatory attack on President Adams in a handbill for which he was convicted in 1800 of libel under the Sedition Act (Chapter 12). He was arrested, fined and imprisoned for six months. During his trial Cooper could not resist pointing out that he knew the King of England could do no wrong, "*but did not know till now that the President of the United States had the same attitude*". Tragically, while Cooper was in prison his wife, Alice, died. Fifty years later Congress remitted the fine on him.

When the Federalists were defeated by the Democrats in the election of 1800 the fortunes of both Priestley and Cooper improved and the political attacks on them abated. This was an immense relief to Priestley and he was able to devote more time at his home in Northumberland, working on his scientific and theological projects. But he was noticeably less healthy and his constant indigestion grew worse. Cooper spent time nursing and caring for him and was with Priestley when he died at his home in January 1804. One of Priestley's final acts was to bequeath his entire library and laboratory to Cooper.

Cooper's Later Career

For his support of the anti-Federalist cause, the Democratic party rewarded Cooper with the district judgeship of northern Pennsylvania in 1804. By all accounts he tried to steer clear of controversy and served the State conscientiously. But he never won the support of the more radical faction of the party which wanted to open the practice of law to people without formal training and to make judges subject to popular election. Cooper opposed the idea and his opponents took an opportunity to remove him from office in 1811 on charges of official misconduct and abuse of authority, charges which he denied. Nevertheless, he was convicted and fined. The experience left Cooper with a more jaundiced view of popular democracy as something "*not quite so perfect in practice as it is beautiful in theory*".[16]

Cooper decided to turn his attention back to science, and in 1811 he was offered the Chair of Chemistry and Mineralogy at Dickinson College at Carlisle, Pennsylvania, which he held until 1815.

He quickly created a very good academic reputation by establishing an excellent chemistry course and by writing articles for the public on various scientific subjects. He also served as a scientific adviser to President James Madison. Unfortunately, the College ran into financial difficulties and Cooper moved on to the University of Pennsylvania where he taught chemistry and

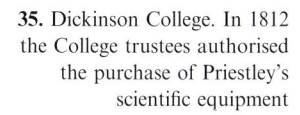

35. Dickinson College. In 1812 the College trustees authorised the purchase of Priestley's scientific equipment

mineralogy. He continued to be a prodigious writer on scientific and legal subjects and became an active member of the American Academy of Natural Sciences and of the American Philosophical Society. In 1812 Cooper also re-married; he and his new wife, Elizabeth Hemming, had three children together.

Cooper had formed a close friendship with Thomas Jefferson and in 1819 he was in line to take up the Chair in Chemistry at the new university the former President had created at Charlottesville in Virginia. However, once more Cooper's radical political and religious opinions proved unacceptable to Virginia's influential religious leaders. He therefore accepted in 1820 a professorship at South Carolina College (now the University of South Carolina). Within a year, he had enlarged his responsibility to geology and mineralogy, and in 1821 he became President of the College, a post he held until 1833.

The early years at South Carolina were particularly successful ones for Cooper. He was popular with the students and, under his guidance, the scientific academic reputation of the College flourished. He advanced the field of medicine and pressed for the formation of a medical school in the South. It was not long however before his outspoken views on several charged issues, notably the rights of the individual States of the Union, attracted criticism. He questioned the benefit of the Union and believed it was an *"unequal alliance"* in which the South would be the perennial loser. He even prophesied that the Union could not endure and he was one of the first and most vocal proponents of the right of individual States to secede from the Union. He also offended the abolitionist campaigners when, despite his earlier opposition to slavery, he changed his mind and doubted whether the rich lands of South Carolina or Georgia could be cultivated without slave labour.

Cooper continued to defend himself skilfully before the College's Board of Trustees against attacks from his enemies. But in 1834 he was finally forced to

36. Thomas Cooper in later life

resign. He was by now a confirmed agnostic and had refused to allow the teaching of religion or theology at the College.

Nonetheless, he remained popular with many of the leading political figures in South Carolina and soon after his resignation from the College, the Governor appointed him to compile and edit all the statute laws of Carolina. However, the days of struggle and controversy were almost over. His health began to fail and he was forced to give up his work on the statutes. In the last few months of his life, he still found time to occupy himself by drawing up a catalogue of the books in his personal library which covered a wonderful range of subjects and interests. Amongst the stock of over 20,000 books were 30 volumes of the work of Joseph Priestley. Thomas Cooper died in May 1839 at the age of 79 and was buried in South Carolina at the Trinity Churchyard in Columbia. The library of the University of South Carolina was named after him in 1976.

Conclusion

From an early age Thomas Cooper was a passionate advocate of political and intellectual freedom. He never held political power, but by force of his personality, courage and intellect, he had significant influence on public affairs, especially in America. He courted controversy and was a most effective agitator against authority, and he suffered for it. In some ways his life was a succession of failures. As he grew older, he left behind his former highly optimistic and idealistic views, and became much more realistic and utilitarian in his outlook, and even pessimistic about the future. When he arrived in America in 1794, he had declared that *"There is little fault with the government of America, either in principle or practice ... the present irritation of men's minds in Great Britain, and the discordant state of society on political grounds is not known here*". However, towards the end of his life, his was disillusioned enough to declare that "*in no country whatever is a spirit of persecution for mere opinions, more prevalent than in the United States of America. It is a country most tolerant in theory and most bigoted in practice*".[17]

Without doubt, Cooper could pursue matters too energetically at times, even for Priestley, for there was a reckless element in Cooper's make-up which made him a difficult, even destructive, person to work with. The friendship between the two men certainly had its problems. But they shared too many of the same fundamental ideals and principles, that relentless search for truth, and love of knowledge, to let such matters upset for long the strength of their relationship. When Priestley died at his home in 1804, it is fitting to know that his friend Thomas Cooper was there with him.

Priestley's influence on Cooper's life extended from the grave. Soon after Priestley's death, Cooper wrote several appendices to the *Memoirs of Dr Joseph Priestley to the year 1795* which were published in 1806. In that work, the study Cooper made of Priestley's great discoveries in chemistry did much to re-kindle his own interest in scientific work.

CHAPTER 10

King George III, William Pitt and Edmund Burke
The Forces of Conservatism

In 1780, Joseph Priestley had left the services of Lord Shelburne and taken up his appointment as a minister at the New Meeting House Chapel in Birmingham. He was at the height of his powers and full of hope for the future. He was internationally famous as a scientist and the acknowledged leader of the liberal reformers, the so-called 'Rational Dissenters'. His family were growing up around him and he was joining in Birmingham a community of like-minded people, not least the eminent group of friends who made up the Lunar Society. He admitted later that the 11 years that he spent at the Chapel were among the happiest and most influential years of his life. But they were also years when storm clouds were gathering around him, and none greater than those unleashed by the French Revolution.

It was also the decade in which Priestley redoubled his efforts to campaign for parliamentary reform and for the rights of the Dissenters. In his characteristically outspoken way, he attacked the Government and the established Church. Already unpopular for his religious views, by the turn of the decade he

37. King George III, William Pitt and Edmund Burke

found himself branded as a dangerous revolutionary and enemy of the State. At the heart of the conservative reaction to his activities were three powerful adversaries – King George III, William Pitt and Edmund Burke – who in combination made a most formidable enemy.

King George III

George III reigned over the British people for 60 years. It is easy to depict him as a stupid, conservative and bigoted monarch who resisted change, lost the American colonies and brought misery to Ireland. There can be no doubt that he was an obstinate and short-sighted man who resolutely opposed reform in whatever form, not least *"Popery"* and Dissent. But he was not a despot. He was typical of many Englishmen of his age. He believed in the superiority of England and in everything English. His chauvinism compelled him to oppose the rebellion of the American colonists and to regard the French as a *"licentious people"*. He prized respectability which made him a good and faithful husband to reportedly a rather dull and ugly wife who bore his 15 legitimate children. However, he was not an uncultured man and was a patron of art and literature, took an interest in science and founded the Royal Academy. He might not have been able to read until he was 11, but he was cleverer than he seemed and had a great sense of duty. He was very conscientious and had a sound grasp of the details of government.

The King was not one to forgive or forget his enemies easily, nor did he disguise his antipathy to other public figures such as John Wilkes and Charles Fox as well as Priestley. Priestley's staunch defence of the American colonists during the American Revolution and his attack on the British government had soon made him most unpopular with the King. Moreover, George III was determined to protect the special position of the Church of England in national life, and the prominent part that Priestley played in pressing for the Dissenters' rights was another good reason the King had for disliking him. Priestley's religious views, in books such as the *History of the Corruptions of Christianity* (1782), and his defence of Unitarianism, convinced the King that he was not only a dangerous radical but also a disgraceful atheist.

Nevertheless, he was not blind to Priestley's ability, and at least before the French Revolution he was prepared to put his prejudice aside to assist a man who was after all a distinguished man of science. This is illustrated in the letter the King wrote in February 1779 when Priestley sought his permission to use the King's Library:

If Dr Priestley applies to my librarian, he will have permission to see the library as other men of science have had; but I cannot think that the Doctor's character as a politician or divine deserves my appearing at all in it; instruments I have none in London. I am sorry that Mr Eden has any intimacy with that Doctor, as I am not over-fond of those that frequent any disciples or companions of the Jesuit in Berkley Square.[1]

(The reference of *Jesuit* is to Lord Shelburne, the Whig politician whom the King distrusted. Priestley was in Shelburne's service at the time.)

However, even the scant regard which the King had for Priestley disappeared once the revolutionary events in France turned to an attack on the monarchy itself. In the summer of 1791, the King's supporters were probably behind a plot to grossly mislead the public by falsely displaying Priestley as a rabid republican set on the execution of the King and the establishment of a republican government. A seditious handbill was printed and distributed in the Midlands showing Priestley as "*Gunpowder Joe*" and toasting the King's head on a charger; simultaneously James Gillray produced a cartoon in London showing the Whigs beheading the King, and Priestley offering comfort to him, "*My dear, brother, we must all die once*".

King George was further outraged by the execution of Louis XVl and Marie Antoinette in 1793. He denounced their executions as the work of savages. From then onwards, Priestley and other sympathisers of the French Revolution were regarded by the King and his supporters as very serious enemies who needed to be suppressed and quickly.

The King fully supported the measures described later in this chapter that his Prime Minister, William Pitt, took in the early 1790s to clamp down on the activities of radicals. What both men feared most of all was that any public agitation would either lead to or provoke riot and mob rule, and they were determined that any outbreak of violence, like the Gordon riots of 1780, had to be cracked down upon at all costs. Thus as much as the King held Priestley and his followers in contempt, the former had no hesitation in condemning the Birmingham riots as the greater evil. He wrote to the Home Secretary (Henry Dundas) following the riots in which Priestley's house and other properties were destroyed:

Though I cannot but feel better pleased that Priestley is the sufferer for the doctrines he and his party have instilled, and that the people see them in their true light, yet I cannot approve their having employed such atrocious means of showing their discontent.[2]

In the years that followed the riots, the King remained a resolute foe of Priestley, although his energies became directed more at opposing any emancipation of the Roman Catholics and propagating the war with France. By the mid-1790s however, the reaction of the country to the mayhem and violence of the French Revolution, together with the repressive measures brought in by Pitt, had meant that radicalism and disorder were effectively under control. To the King's satisfaction he saw the "*heretic*" Priestley driven from the land.

38. Gillray cartoon of Priestley calling for the Head of George III

39. Doctor Phlogiston or Political Priest expounds his incendiary views

There was a surge of popular support for the King as the Father of the People, and as the defender of the British Empire and all Europe against Napoleon Bonaparte. But in 1811 the King's health broke down permanently, and in the following year his eldest son, the Prince of Wales, became Regent and succeeded his father to the throne as George IV in 1820.

William Pitt

In William Pitt the Younger, Priestley faced a more astute and political opponent than King George III. As we shall see later, maybe Priestley's relationship with Pitt never quite reached the level of bitterness that he came to feel for his former friend Edmund Burke. However, it was Pitt's repressive measures, his so-called *"Reign of Terror"* that effectively crushed the hopes of the Dissenters and the other reform bodies.

Pitt served as Prime Minister in momentous times. He led his country through the French Revolution and the subsequent Napoleonic Wars. His achievements were considerable and he was a hero of the propertied middle class. He restored the financial health of the country, attacked corruption and governed the country efficiently. His political battles with Fox and the Whigs were historic especially during the time of the King's *"madness"*.

It is difficult to assess Pitt's character and personality. Very ambitious and arrogant, he seemed to love power for its own sake. Many people found him aloof and few men were drawn to him. His manner at the Treasury Bench in the House of Commons was described by a contemporary as being cold, stiff and without suavity or amenity. Fundamentally Tory in his political views, he regarded himself as an independent Whig. He had great administrative ability, an unremitting attention to work and high personal integrity. He had a very practical approach to public affairs and provided a stable government much less factious and corrupt than its predecessors. But he drank heavily and was always in debt. Prepared to commit himself in principle to reform, he was still ready

40. Gillray print of 1803 portrays George III as a huntsman holding Napoleon's head to a pack of hounds with collars inscribed with the names of famous war leaders such as Nelson. In the background Pitt leads a group of men galloping towards the King

to vote and work against it if he felt that the timing and details were mistaken. To sum up, he was a cautious man but could resort to harsh methods when required.

When Pitt became Prime Minister at the age of 24 in 1783, Priestley believed that the chances of relief for Dissenters and political reform generally had taken a real turn for the better. Pitt had established a reputation as a reformer and the Dissenters looked to him for support. However, Priestley was bitterly disillusioned when in March 1787 Pitt failed to support a motion brought before Parliament to repeal the Test and Corporation Acts. Pitt seemingly opposed the measure on mainly pragmatic grounds that the timing was wrong.

Priestley, who had listened to all the Parliamentary speeches, was most offended by Pitt's evasiveness and his contention that if the Dissenters were allowed relief then they would simply ask for more, and saw his stance as a dishonourable betrayal. He immediately wrote a scathing letter in protest to Pitt. Imprudently, he couched his concerns in a high handed tone that succeeded in not only annoying the young Prime Minister but also upsetting some of Priestley's own Dissenting supporters.

In his letter, Priestley also tried repair the damage done earlier by the caricature of him as *Gunpowder Joe, the Priestley Politician or the Political Priest*. He explained to Pitt that the means that the Dissenters proposed to employ were not force but persuasion and *"The gunpowder which we are so assiduously laying grain by grain under the old building of error and superstition ... is not composed of saltpetre, charcoal and sulphur, but consists of arguments"*. He went on to demand that the universities should be opened up to Dissenters, clerical seats in the House of Lords should be reduced, and that Dissenters should not be forced to contribute to the maintenance of the established Church. He sneered at Pitt's subservience to the Bishops who, he said, were *"recorded in all histories as the most jealous, the most timorous, and of course, the most vindictive of men"*. He finished by sharply reminding Pitt that the people had been led by him to expect a reform in parliamentary representation but as yet there was no sign of it.[3]

Not surprisingly, the letter had the effect of hardening conservative opposition to the Dissenters' cause, and especially from the Anglican Church. Consequently, when Priestley and his supporters made a further attempt in 1789 to repeal the Test and Corporation Acts they found that opposition in cities such as Leeds, Manchester and Birmingham was better organised and more influential than before.

On 1 March 1789, the day before Parliament was to debate yet again the petition to repeal the Acts, MPs received a series of printed extracts of Priestley's latest writings which gave the impression that there was indeed an imminent danger of a gunpowder plot. Fox, who was proposing the motion for repeal, did his best to show that Priestley in fact posed no threat to the State or

41. A cartoon of 1790 showing two men arguing vehemently about the Test laws. The man on the left points to the paper – "The Rights of the Church maintained" – whilst on the right the man holds a paper marked "the conduct of the dissenters vindicated"

to the Church. However, he faced powerful parliamentary opponents, notably Edmund Burke, who made full use of the misleading material to mount a malevolent attack on Priestley and his Dissenter friends. Burke alleged that young Dissenters were being taught by Richard Price and Theophilus Lindsey to renounce Church and King, and reminded the House of Priestley's infamous gunpowder letter. This, he said, confirmed Priestley's determination *"to proceed, step by step, till the whole of the Church Establishment was levelled to its foundations"*.[4]

Pitt, characteristically, stayed aloof from the debate and said little beyond offering some mild rebuke for Priestley and Bishop Horsley, and the motion was subsequently heavily defeated. The defeat marked a severe set-back for the Dissenters' cause. The conservative so-called *Church and King* party had asserted its power, and thereafter its influence gathered momentum. With the outbreak of the French Revolution, the Dissenters' influence further declined, and they lost any chance of winning the legal relief they sought until well into the nineteenth century.

The French Revolution
The Revolution in France in 1789 changed everything. At first it was widely welcomed by conservatives and reformers in England. Pitt approved the downfall of a despotic and corrupt regime and even the arch conservative Burke gave it a guarded reception. Within two years however attitudes had been transformed. Whilst liberals and reformers like Priestley remained convinced that the Revolution heralded the beginning of a modern age in which happiness, liberty and equality would flourish, conservatives came to view the Revolution as simply the most dangerous enemy that ever disturbed the peace of the world.

In 1791, Priestley wrote a pamphlet defending the Revolution. He argued that he believed the outcome would eventually lead to *"universal peace and goodwill among nations"*, and would make possible an *"empire of reason"*. King George

42. Storming of the Bastille on 14 July 1789. The Symbol of the French Revolution. When it fell it held only seven prisoners

III and Pitt had little trouble with those sentiments but they were much more alarmed when Priestley went on to predict that in future monarchs will be *"first servants of the people and accountable to them"*.[5] The problem however for Priestley and other reformers was that as events in France took a more sinister and threatening turn, their comparatively mild reform agenda became inextricably mixed in the eyes of the authorities with the more extreme views of some of the revolutionary societies and clubs. Inevitably, prominent radicals and Dissenters like Priestley found themselves the target for attack.

Throughout this period, Priestley would have been well advised to moderate some of his wilder views but he was not to be subdued. He stubbornly believed in the inherent good of the French Revolution and continued to press publicly for more liberty and political reform. He even abandoned some of his earlier regard for the institutions of King, Lords and Commons in favour of a more republican form of government. And, despite all the protestations from Priestley and his friends that the Dissenters were not intent on violence, their use of inflammatory words suggested otherwise. They were accused of being traitors plotting treason, spreading radical notions and corrupting the minds of the ignorant and unthinking. Some very far-fetched accusations were thrown about; in Liverpool, for example, it was claimed that Dissenting radicals consisted of *"schoolmasters and unitarian preachers of different Sectaries such as Presbyterians, Quakers and Jews"*.[6]

Pitt's "Reign of Terror"
Pitt, like the King, became increasingly alarmed that France was intent on a concerted attempt to spread its revolutionary Jacobinism to Britain and the rest of Europe. The political unrest that broke out in Britain in the early 1790s confirmed their worst fears that the country was indeed on the brink of violence and revolution. On the face of it, there was plenty of evidence to support their fears. Anti-establishment propaganda had been given a huge boost by Thomas Paine's famous publication in 1791, *The Declaration of the Rights of Man*, with its anti-monarchy and pro-revolutionary principles. The book was sold in tens of thousands; it was claimed that Paine's book *"is now made a Standard book in this Country as Robinson Crusoe and the Pilgrim's Progress"*.[7] Alarmingly, there were also outbreaks of violence across the country. Apart from the Birmingham riots of 1791, other disturbances broke out in cities such as Sheffield, Manchester and Leicester.

Inspired by the course of events in France, the newly formed Constitutional societies and clubs also pressed ahead with their programmes for political reform. The Sheffield Society for Constitutional Information led the way in 1791, closely followed by the London Corresponding Society. Although both were run mainly by artisans committed to democracy and parliamentary reform, by 1793 ever more radical ideas began to spread rapidly throughout the land, spurred on by grievances over food prices and wages, and the spread of extremist pamphlets and newspapers.

Fearful that events were drifting out of control, government supporters demanded action. Pitt decided to move quickly to counter the threat of radical bodies and their publications. In May and December 1792 two royal proclamations were issued against *"seditious writings"* and the government began rounding up prominent radicals. The leaders of the London radical societies were soon arrested for trial. And in Scotland, particularly hard sentences were imposed by the judges, and in 1793 after the trial of the *"Reform Martyrs"*, Thomas Muir and others were transported to Botany Bay.

In 1794, the Habeas Corpus Act was suspended making it possible for people to be detained in prison without trial. Spies for the government continued to keep a close watch on the activities of reformers, including Priestley, and since the spies were paid piece work they had an incentive to concoct exaggerated accounts. Several reformers were driven from the country. Joseph Gales for example, the Unitarian editor of the influential radical newspaper, the *Sheffield Register* and founder-member of the Sheffield Constitutional Society, fled to America to avoid arrest. Priestley's friend, Theophilus Lindsey, likened the exodus of radical Dissenters to America in the early 1790s to that of the Puritans in the days of Archbishop Laud.

Pitt realised the importance of mobilising and exploiting public support for his measures, notably from the middle and upper classes. Although he was reluctant to create more public associations, he quickly seized on the support of the *Association for the Preservation of Liberty and Property against Republicans and Levellers* which had been founded in 1792 by a government officer, John Reeves. The *Association* ideally suited Pitt's purpose since it appealed strongly to the propertied and merchant classes. It would, he remarked, provide the impression and effect of numbers on our side without the danger of too much public agitation.[8] Without doubt, the emergence of small but influential groups of local men acting in the name of the public interest to counter radicals suited Pitt, the politician, perfectly. Within months many hundreds of these loyalist organisations had been established and they proved to be remarkably successful in curbing the activities of radicals at the local level.

By the middle of the 1790s Pitt's repressive measures had been successful in curbing the radical movement and its leaders had been dispersed or driven underground. However, Pitt's so-called *Reign of Terror* can be exaggerated since there were only 200 prosecutions over a period of ten years and charges were often dropped. The new measures were only temporary and a state of absolute tyranny was well beyond the modest resources of the Home Office. Nonetheless, many people did suffer badly and the repressive measures undoubtedly succeeded in frightening some of the radical societies out of existence. On the other hand, the heavy handed measures simply antagonised others who became even more determined in due course to bring about radical reform.[9]

43. William Pitt on the search for revolutionaries

44. Gillray cartoon showing Pitt steering a boat, *The Constitution*, between the Rock of Democracy and the Whirlpool of Arbitrary Power, and towards a castle flying a flag inscribed "Haven of Democracy". Pitt is pursued by Priestley and the Whigs Fox and Sheridan – the sharks or dogs of Scylla

By the end of the 1790s the Prime Minister faced a different set of problems. The war with France was a grave burden on the country, inflation was high, and there was also trouble in Ireland stirred up by the French. In 1798, Irish nationalists attempted a rebellion. In 1801, Pitt's Act of Union brought Britain and Ireland together into one legislative body, and in order to ensure a lasting settlement, Pitt promised the Irish free trade and the emancipation of Roman Catholics. But King George III and political forces opposed the emancipation, fearing that it would threaten the established Church. Pitt offered his resignation to the King who let him go, later described by Lord Macaulay as a case of genius giving way to madness.

Pitt was recalled as Prime Minister in 1804 to form a Grand Alliance against France, and for most of his remaining years as Prime Minister his energies were consumed by fighting the war against France. He was filled with hope of ending the war after Nelson's victory at Trafalgar in 1805, but his hopes were shattered by Napoleon's victory at Austerlitz in December 1805 over Russia and Austria. Pitt's health broken, he died in 1806, probably of renal failure and cirrhosis of the liver, at the age of 46. His final words were said to be "*Oh, my country! How I leave my country!*".[10] Other versions of his last words exist, including "*How I love my country*" and "*Oh, what times! Oh, my country!*". Benjamin Disraeli preferred the version taken allegedly from an old doorkeeper of the House of Commons, "*I think I could eat one of Bellamy's pork pies*".

Edmund Burke

The French Revolution also drove the third of our protagonists, Edmund Burke, into a fierce conflict with Joseph Priestley and his supporters.

Edmund Burke was a very influential Anglo-Irish political thinker, politician and orator with, it has been claimed, perhaps, *"the largest mind ever given to politics in these islands"*.[11] With Disraeli, he is renowned as one of the fathers of modern conservative thinking. He accepted that, from time to time, reform was necessary but it should be reform that would preserve and strengthen a country's history, institutions and its traditions and not destroy them. He was not necessarily against political theory, but it needed to have stood the test of time, and not *"weak, erroneous, fallacious, unfounded theory"*.[12] But he could also be hard and vindictive; to the famous feminist, Mary Wollstonecraft, Burke was as *"a venal opportunist"* who, she claimed, had once gathered statistics from asylums to prove George III clearly mad so that his son, the future Prince Regent, could seize power and make him paymaster general.[13]

Burke studied for the law but he was never called to the Bar, and spent some years travelling about and earning a living from his writing. He also made some significant and influential friendships such as Samuel Johnson and Oliver Goldsmith. Edward Gibbon described him as *"the most eloquent and rational madman that I ever knew"*.[14] He married Jane Nugent in 1757, the daughter of a Catholic physician. Jane apparently had *"a mild, reasonable and obliging manner"* which could soothe the excitable temperament of her husband. Ambitious, he entered Parliament in 1766 and joined the Whig party. In his early years he took a clear liberal stance on a number of issues and, at that time, Burke was enjoying a good relationship with Priestley. During the American Revolution Burke came round to the view that it would be wiser to allow the colonists to have their independence, and Priestley and his friends were impressed with the strong stand he took on this issue against both the King and Parliament. He also campaigned tirelessly for the emancipation of Catholics and against the abuse of power and cruelties of the East India Company.

However, it was the Dissenters' campaign for the repeal of the Test and Corporation Acts that signalled the end of his friendship with Priestley. Burke had previously been in favour of repeal, but once the French Revolution began to unfold, he moved sharply to the right; when Fox proposed yet again in May 1792 the repeal of the Acts, Burke used the occasion to oppose strongly the cause of the Dissenters in the House of Commons. He argued against relief on the grounds that the political circumstances had changed, and that Fox and the Dissenters were perversely influenced by abstract discussion of political rights. He asserted that he had come to distrust deeply slogans such as *"The rights of man"* and all those philosophers, agitators and lawyers who engaged in politics. In short, his old friends had become his enemies.

In his parliamentary attack, Burke singled out particularly the Unitarians, comparing them to loathsome insects that unless crushed would grow into giant spiders as large as oxen, building iron webs that would catch everyone who opposed them. Price (although now dead) and Priestley were named as dangerous men, traitors to the English Constitution and its freedoms. This attack, coming from a man thought of earlier by many liberals as *"A Friend of the People"*, hurt Priestley deeply and was one he could not forgive. Shortly before he fled to America he wrote to the *Morning Chronicle* pointing out that *"When Mr Burke and I were acquainted, and we used to converse on the subject of politics ... our sentiments respecting the Constitution, and the principles of liberty in general were, as I then conceived, the same"*.[15]

The Reflections

Burke had been particularly outraged by Richard Price's famous sermon in 1789, *Discourse on the Love of our Country*, which asserted the natural rights of man and concluded with those words that *"all ye oppressors of the world"* should tremble (Chapter 3). He was also alarmed by a letter he had received around the same time from another of his former friends, the radical pamphleteer Thomas Paine. Paine had written enthusiastically, but unwittingly, to him from France that the Revolution was *"certainly the Forerunner to other revolutions in Europe"*.[16]

The response of Burke was to write his famous work, *Reflections on the Revolution in France*, published in November 1790, which pronounced in eloquent terms the conservative case. The book is based on the premise that fundamental change is dangerous unless it accords with a country's history and traditions. The real problem, he argued, with revolutionaries like Price and

45. Frontispiece to Burke's *Reflections on the French Revolution* (1790). Burke is on bended knee proposing to a vision of Marie Antoinette while a cherub touches his head with a firebrand with sparks of romance

Priestley was their presumptuous demands for simplicity which led them to renounce the past and to break up all the solid links that held society together socially. And like the King and Pitt, Burke much feared the passions of the mob and decided that the country must be warned against the dangers it faced. He roundly condemned the Revolution in France as the beginning of mob rule by the "*swinish multitude*", and prophesied that it would lead inevitably to instability and violence. Although Priestley is not named specifically in the *Reflections*, there is no doubt that he was uppermost in Burke's mind. Everyone knew just to whom he was referring when he described the Revolution as the "*wild gas, the fixed air, is plainly broken loose*". Burke maintained that any judgement on the Revolution needed to be suspended, "*until we see something deeper than the agitation of a troubled and frothy surface*".[17]

At first the *Reflections* attracted little interest, but once the Revolution had worsened, alarm broke out among the propertied classes and other conservative elements in Britain. Before long the dire prophecies Burke had made in the *Reflections* appeared only too true and Burke emerged as the spokesman for the counter revolution. The work effectively polarised public opinion in Britain. A massive and prolonged pamphlet war broke out between the liberal and conservative camps, which has left us with a political vocabulary still very much in use today. Words such as liberal, conservative, equality, fraternity, socialist, anarchy and capitalism can all trace their roots to this period.

The *Reflections* struck a chord in the nation and attracted much acclaim. Eleven editions were prepared within a year and around 30,000 copies sold. The King described it as "*a very good book; every gentleman ought to read it*".[18] Edward Gibbon, an avowed atheist, was full of praise for Burke's views which he commented could almost excuse the latter's reverence for Church establishment. And Catherine, the Empress of Russia, sent her congratulations to Burke for denouncing French philosophers as miscreants and wretches.

However, the book also aroused a lot of hostility. Major attacks were launched on Burke between 1790 and 1792, among the most important were Mary Wollstonecraft's *A Vindication of the Rights of Man* (1790) and Thomas Paine's *Rights of Man* (1792) which argued for a fully republican style of government. Priestley's own response came in his *Letters to Burke* published in January 1791. He declared his surprise and disappointment at Burke's work, and regretted that he could no longer class Burke "*among the friends of what I deem to be the cause of liberty, civil or religious*". He censured Burke's work as being "*not to be sufficiently cool ... and your imagination is evidently heated and your ideas confused*".[19]

In the years that followed, Burke advocated war with France and the crushing of the French Republic. He persisted in personally attacking Priestley and his supporters at every opportunity. Priestley was annoyed that on several occasions Burke had used the House of Commons to attack him, "*a place where*

46. Print showing Edmund Burke as Don Quixote, wearing armor, carrying lance and shield labeled "Shield of Aristocracy and Despotism"

he knows I cannot reply to him, and from which he also knows that his accusation will reach every corner of the country and consequently thousands of persons who will never read any writings of mine". Burke sought even to discredit Priestley's scientific reputation by arguing that science itself was a threat to the established order, and that men of science were amongst other free thinking men who were responsible for the French Revolution. In a clear reference to Priestley, he derided British radicals as being no more than philosophers *"who considered man in their experiments no more than they do mice in an air pump"*. He also took care to remind people of Priestley's earlier reference to *"gunpowder"* which, Burke argued, proved conclusively that science itself was linked to sedition.[20]

It was populist rhetoric like Burke's that was used to exploit the ugly feelings in Birmingham towards the Dissenters and to stir up the drunken mob which destroyed Priestley's home in July 1791. Burke was in Margate at the time, and it was said that he was *"elated"* when the news of the riots reached him.

Following the execution of Louis XVI in January 1793, Burke and other conservatives took the opportunity to redouble attacks in Parliament and elsewhere on Dissenters, and a new wave of violence erupted against them and their sympathisers. Priestley believed that his life and that of his family were in real danger. For some time he was not able to walk outside his house without seeing effigies of himself strung up from the gallows or portrayed as a wolf or a shark. With his friends being deported to Botany Bay or jailed, he knew it was only a matter of time before he too would be punished. He accepted that the time had come for him and his family to leave Britain and to sail for the New World.

Burke remained an implacable enemy of revolutionary France until his death in July 1797 and opposed any move to recognise the French government. He continued to attack his critics and to deplore the condition of his native Ireland. But his final years were overshadowed by the loss of his only son, Richard, on whom his ambitions rested. The Whig leader, Charles Fox, proposed that Burke's body should be placed amongst the illustrious dead of Westminster Abbey. However, Burke had made it clear that his burial should be private and he was laid to rest in a little church in Beaconsfield.

Conclusion
In the end, Priestley's refusal to moderate his religious and political views at a time when most of the country feared revolution and invasion brought him down. His departure for America along with other prominent radical reformers dealt a severe blow to the reform movement and its organisation. The loss of its leaders, combined with the impact of censorship, intimidation and penal measures, left it isolated and without a sense of direction. The excesses of the French Revolution and the outbreak of a long war with France also greatly helped the conservative cause for it restrained many would-be reformers who had previously looked to France for inspiration. And throughout the country, anti-radical propaganda and the formation of the loyalist associations effectively mobilised public opinion against any form of radicalism. King George, Pitt and Burke had good reason for satisfaction. One of their chief adversaries had fled the land and, for the time being at least, the forces of conservatism were triumphant.

CHAPTER 11

William Cobbett
(1763–1835)
The People's Tribune

When Joseph Priestley stepped onto the quay at New York harbour on 4 June 1794 he had good reason to be pleased. He and his wife had survived a particularly rough and unpleasant voyage across the Atlantic and they looked forward to joining their two sons, Joseph and William, who had already settled in America. And perhaps more importantly, having been driven from England by persecution and renewed threats of violence, they yearned now for a period of peace and quiet.

News of the imminent arrival of the famous Dr Priestley had gripped America where he was held in high esteem. As well as his scientific reputation,

47. William Cobbett

Priestley was well-known in America for his support during the American Revolution and his defence of the liberties of the new Republic. On his arrival in New York he was given a very warm welcome to the *"shores of Liberty and Equality"*. Honours were showered upon Priestley, and within a day or so of his arrival the principal citizens of New York, along with deputations from several learned and political societies, had come to greet him and to pay their respects. He wrote to Theophilus Lindsay that *"Almost every person of consequence in the place has been, or is coming, to call upon me"*.[1] The *American Daily Advertiser* declared that *"The name of Joseph Priestley will be long remembered among all enlightened people; and there is no doubt that England will one day regret her ungrateful treatment to this venerable and illustrious man ... His arrival in this city calls upon us to testify our respect and esteem for a man whose whole life has been devoted to the sacred duty of diffusing knowledge and happiness among nations"*.[2]

Although all this euphoria was not entirely to Priestley's liking, he responded publicly to his welcome by rejoicing *"in finding an asylum from persecution in a country in which ... abuses have come to a natural termination"*.[3]

In the days that followed, he stressed that he hoped to continue without fear of molestation in what remained of his life by *"advancing the cause of science, of virtue and of religion"*.[4] He was also heartened by the prospects for the Unitarian faith, especially in American colleges, and to his Unitarian friend Thomas Belsham, back in England, he confided that *"The harvest truly is ready, and you must send us labourers"*.[5]

Such optimism was sadly premature. Despite the rapturous reception he had received in New York and Philadelphia, his political reputation and his radical democratic and Francophile opinions were bound to arouse prejudice against him amongst those who sided more with Britain, especially at a time when political passions were running high in the new Republic. It was not long before he was writing to Theophilus Lindsey that *"nobody asked me to preach, and I hear there is much jealousy and dread of me"*.[6] More ominously, within a few months of his arrival his peace of mind was to be shattered by the start of public persecution of him by Peter Porcupine, the pen name of a fellow countryman who had also fled from England, William Cobbett. For the next six years the formidable Porcupine was to become Dr Priestley's tenacious enemy and chief tormentor.

William Cobbett was born in Farnham, Surrey, in 1763, and led an extraordinarily adventurous and varied life. He was by nature a conservative but with radical opinions, and he was to become the leading political commentator of his age. He was famous for rooting out corruption in public affairs, and for seeking radical solutions to the economic and social distresses of the labouring classes, especially the agricultural. He came to represent the passing of Old England and championed traditional ways of life against the changes brought about by the Industrial Revolution. During his lifetime almost every notable person in England, France and the United States was attacked by him. John Stuart Mill thought that there were two sorts of people he could not endure: those who differed from him and those who agreed with him. He always thought the latter stole his ideas. He liked labelling people with sardonic nicknames and he even dismissed the venerable Benjamin Franklin as an *"old lightning rod"*.[7] A prolific and aggressive pamphleteer, he was convicted several times for libel and sedition in both Britain and America.

Cobbett's Early Life
The son of an inn-keeper and small-time farmer, Cobbett started his working life as a ploughboy and crow scarer. At the age of 19, he decided to seek adventure by joining the Army. He spent most of his leisure hours on self improvement, learning English grammar and reading the English classics. Soon promoted, he went with his regiment to Nova Scotia in Canada. On leaving the Army in 1791, he charged some of his officers with corruption but, when they sought to bring counter charges against him, he fled to France with his newly wed wife, Anne. Although happy there, he realised that revolutionary France was not a safe place for an Englishman, so he and his wife decided to leave for America in 1792.

Cobbett settled in Philadelphia where he supported himself and his family by teaching English to French émigrés and by writing. As a natural agitator, it was inevitable that the sensation and publicity surrounding Priestley's arrival in

48. Cobbett – Ploughboy to Army

America would be likely to attract Cobbett's attention, and the more famous the man the better. In 1794 he was to write the famous pamphlet attacking Joseph Priestley which effectively launched his career as a formidable journalist.

Priestley's friends had warned him to keep clear of political debate at a time when political tensions between the Federalist Party, which inclined towards support for Britain, and the pro-French and anti-British Democratic Party were running high. Perhaps if he had simply expressed his gratitude for the welcoming addresses he had received and moved quickly on to establishing his new home in Pennsylvania, he would probably have avoided Cobbett's attention. But Priestley sympathised naturally with the views of the Democratic Party and it was his response to the welcoming address of the American Democratic Societies which caused the trouble. Although Priestley stopped short of actually endorsing the Societies, he could not resist openly supporting many of their sentiments. He praised the wisdom of republican governments and condemned the wrongdoings of monarchical ones. He lamented the degenerate and tyrannical state of Europe, and declared his unequivocal preference for the governance of America to that of Britain.

The Porcupine's Attack
When one of Cobbett's students showed him the article in a newspaper reprinting the fulsome addresses to Priestley on his arrival together with the latter's replies, Cobbett's anger was aroused. He instinctively reacted against any criticism of the British Crown and Constitution, especially when it came from a fellow countryman, and he resolved to write and publish his pamphlet in defence of his country. Written under his pen name Peter Porcupine, his pamphlet *Observations on the Emigration of Dr Joseph Priestley*, was unquestionably a slanderous and often illogical piece of work. Nonetheless, it was an impressive piece of writing, expressed in his typically straightforward, bold and polemical language, and overnight it captured the public imagination and attention.

Cobbett showed no respect at all for Priestley or his achievements. He knew nothing of science and was contemptuous of all forms of non-conformity. His objective was to expose Priestley not as a political refugee fleeing from repression, nor someone seeking religious freedom, but as a traitor to his King and country and enemy of the established Church. He warned Americans of the danger of such a man whom he branded as both a knave and a fool.

The following extracts illustrate how Cobbett mocked and satirised Priestley. Although himself lacking any formal education, he did not hesitate to open up an attack on the learned Doctor's writing ability. Thus he wrote:

As to his talents as a writer we have only to open our eyes to be convinced that they are far below mediocrity. His style is uncouth and superlatively diffuse. Always involved in minutiae, every sentence is a string of parenthesis, in finding the end of which, the reader is lucky if he does not lose the proposition they were meant to illustrate. In short, the whole of his phraseology is extremely disgusting; to which may be added that even in point of grammar he is very often incorrect.[8]

He went on to accuse Priestley of hypocrisy whose "*canting profession of Moderation (was) in direct contradiction to the conduct of his whole Life*".[9] Pointing to Priestley's fervour for the French Revolution, he wondered whether Priestley might not be pleased to see the massacre of an entire race. It was clear, Cobbett maintained, that parliamentary reform was never Priestley's real object, and that his revolutionary doctrines and inflammatory speeches were really an attempt to undermine the laws which the government had made to protect people from violence. On the contrary, claimed Cobbett, Priestley had set out to provoke violence and had only himself to blame for the actions of the Birmingham mob that had destroyed his home.

It was Priestley's and the Democratic Societies' anti-British comments which attracted the full venom of Cobbett's tirade. As a typical "John Bull" with a deep love for his country, he relished the opportunity to take on those who attacked Britain and who sided with France. He warned the Societies that:

Of all the English arrived in these States no one was ever calculated to render them less service than Doctor Priestley; ... his preference for the American government is all affectation: his emigration was not voluntary: he [stayed] in England till he saw no hopes of recovering a lost reputation; and then, bursting with envy and resentment, he fled into what the Tammany society very justly call "banishment", covered with the universal detestation of his countrymen.[10]

Moving on to attack Dr Priestley's religious views, Cobbett claimed that the Doctor might profess toleration and liberty of conscience but his actions and writings suggested otherwise. He drew attention to the fact that Priestley's students in Hackney had been told "*that the established church must fall*", and that in an address to the Jews Priestley had asserted that all the persecutions of the Jews have arisen from Trinitarian, that is to say "*Idolatrous Christians!*". Cobbett exclaimed that:

It is the first time I believe these two words were ever joined together. Is this the language of a man who wanted only toleration, in a country where the established church, and the most part of the dissenters also, are professedly Trinitarians?[11]

Even Priestley's reputation as a philosopher and scientist did not escape Cobbett's criticism. He was contemptuous of both, and in the third edition of the pamphlet he went as far as suggesting that Priestley had plagiarised the results of one of his experiments, and that he had fled from England to escape his *"lost reputation"* as a philosopher.[12]

In America, Cobbett's pamphlet had a mixed reception. The Democrats and those who supported France deplored it, while the Federalists or government party applauded the author as a staunch defender of law and order. It did however prove sufficiently popular to run into five editions in total by 1796. When first published in England, many of Priestley's old enemies were delighted and it was reviewed favourably in the *Gentlemen's Magazine* and in the *British Critic*. Other journals however were more critical and condemned Peter Porcupine as *"a contemptible wretch"* for using such *"Billingsgate abuse"* and *"pitiful attempt at wit"* in the pamphlet, and for its gross and unfair insults of Priestley.[13]

Priestley for once heeded the advice of his friends not to be drawn into controversy, and decided not to be provoked by the pamphlet. He made no public response. Nevertheless, privately, he could not disguise the fact that he was deeply upset and annoyed by the personal attack on him. Unhappily, it also inflamed the prejudice some people, including the clergy, had already formed against him; much to his disappointment, he found that more American pulpits were becoming barred to him.

As for Cobbett, he relished the fame and notoriety that his *Observations* had brought him and this encouraged him to embark fully on a career as a pamphleteer. His writing sold well. Over the next six years he had a meteoric rise to fame and became influential in moulding public opinion in America. From 1794 to 1800, he published some 20 pamphlets criticising various aspects of American political and public life, of which more than 20 million copies were sold in America and Britain. Not content with that, in 1797 he launched a provocative daily newspaper, *Porcupine's Gazette*, with the express intention of *"annihilating, if possible, the intriguing, wicked, and indefatigable faction which the French had formed in this country"*.[14]

Cobbett used the *Gazette* as his main vehicle for relentlessly pursuing his attacks on Priestley. For some time Priestley continued to ignore them, at least publicly. However, he was only too aware of the damage that they were doing to his reputation, and never underestimated the power and popular appeal of Cobbett's writings. He confided in a letter to Lindsey in 1797 that *"Cobbett has more encouragement than any other writer in this country. He, every day, advertizes his [Newspaper] against me, and after my name adds 'commonly known by the name of the fire-brand philosopher'"*.[15]

The Storm Intensifies
In 1798, Cobbett seized a golden opportunity to mount a particularly vitriolic attack on Priestley. A package of letters marked for *"Dr Priestley in America"* had been captured by the British navy on board a Danish vessel and were later published in London. The letters were written in Paris from a long-standing

William Cobbett

Good Master Young,
 I cannot send the whole amount
  With Christian patience watch and wait;
 Take fifty dollars on account,
  And give the bearer a receipt.
                          Wm Cobbett.

P.S. Though I know it is very difficult to rhyme a presbyterian out of his money, yet when in the measure of Watts's psalms, rhyme ought to have some weight. — I will discharge the rest of your bill as soon as possible which, I hope, will be before Saturday night.
Monday, 5 Feb. 1798

49. Peter Porcupine – Cobbett as Editor

Unitarian friend of Priestley called John Hurford Stone. The content of the letters, written to both Priestley and to his friend Benjamin Vaughan also living in America, seriously compromised Priestley's reputation. In the letters, Stone expressed satisfaction with French military conquests in Europe as a result of which, *"The spirit of Equality which has retraversed the Alps, has also entered the Rhine"*. Ominously, he went on to say that preparations were well advanced for an invasion of England, and that *"Whatever can tend to humble the English government is most anxiously sought after, in whatever shape the mode of opposition presents itself"*.[16] Even more alarming was the fact that Stone in his letter to Vaughan requested him specifically to send some supplies of potash to France, an ingredient well-known for making gunpowder.

When news of the letters reached Cobbett he lost no time in publishing his *Gazette* under the sensational title *"PRIESTLEY COMPLETELY DETECTED"*. The letters were published in full along with some withering comments from Cobbett who declared that his portrayal of Priestley as a traitor had now been fully vindicated. He castigated Priestley as a French agent plotting in America with other spies to disunite the people from their government. He insisted that President Adams must deport him, for if *"this discovery passes unnoticed by the government, it will operate as the greatest encouragement that its enemies have ever received"*.[17]

This time Priestley felt sufficiently provoked enough to point out to Cobbett that Stone had written to him as a friend of many years' standing and as a member of his congregation in Hackney. In no way, he asserted, could he be held answerable for the opinions expressed in the letter. But the damage had been done and Cobbett's remarks received widespread publicity. His demand that President Adams should deport Priestley received support amongst the public and in government circles (Chapter 12). Priestley again tried to ride out the storm but he admitted to Lindsey that the furore over the letters and Cobbett's attack on him meant that *"so violent … is party spirit in this country, and so general the prejudice against me as a friend of France, that if there be not a change soon I cannot expect to live in peace here"*.[18] To make matters worse, Priestley had already upset the Adams administration by his criticism of its centralising and undemocratic tendencies. He realised it was a particularly dangerous time for him. The Aliens and Sedition Acts had just been passed in America, and Priestley got wind of the fact that men close to the President Adams were beginning to think the Acts might indeed be applicable to him (Chapter 12).

The President resisted calls for Priestley to be deported but did warn him to keep clear of politics lest he should get into difficulty. If Cobbett's persecution of him had relented Priestley might well have heeded this advice. However, in August 1799, Cobbett again expressed his contempt for Priestley by republishing Hurford Stone's intercepted letters in the *Gazette*. He exploited to the full, and in damaging detail, the activities of Hurford's brother, William, who was another radical friend of Priestley, together with a description of William's subsequent trial in England for high treason. Priestley, in exasperation, was at last driven to respond publicly in an attempt to clear his name.

Priestley Responds

Priestley's response took the form of his publication, *Letters to the Inhabitants of Northumberland (Pennsylvania)*, published in 1799 (Chapter 12). Unfortunately, the publication vindicated the earlier warnings to Priestley that it would be better for him to remain quiet and keep clear of American politics. Far from reassuring people that he was not the dangerous person as branded by Cobbett, the *Letters* played into the hands of Priestley's enemies. The frankness with which Priestley admitted to his political and some other activities whilst in America, indeed some of which he had earlier denied, together with the attack he made on aspects of the American constitution and public life, alarmed and distressed his friends and supporters in both America and Britain. Cobbett himself lost no time in mocking Priestley for the things he now found wrong in America, and urged him to admit his mistake and to return to England.

However, the worst was over. Priestley's publication sold well, and he felt able to write to Lindsey that he believed that the *Letters* had done good and had impressed many who had written to him. He was delighted to receive an appreciative reply from the then Vice-President, Thomas Jefferson, who took the opportunity to sympathise with Priestley over the distress he had endured over the years, commenting "*How deeply have I been chagrined and mortified at the persecutions which fanaticism and monarchy have excited against you, even here*".[19]

By the end of the century, Cobbett's aggressive remarks had succeeded in upsetting many others besides Priestley. Always ambivalent towards America, now even its very institutions and society were not safe from Cobbett's attack wherever he saw misdeeds or the abuse of power. He once described the Americans as, "*a cheating, sly, roguish gang*".[20] He periodically pointed out American shortcomings such as the "*great depravity and corruption of their morals*", the low level of their literacy and the poor quality of their officials.[21] Cobbett soon found himself with more enemies than friends. Political and public opinion moved against him and the readership of his newspaper fell away. He was frequently in conflict with the law; in 1797 he had been prosecuted for having published libels on several political antagonists, including Priestley.

In December 1799, Cobbett found himself in very serious trouble. One of Philadelphia's most distinguished citizens, Dr Benjamin Rush, whom Cobbett had with some justification condemned as a "*poisonous trans-Atlantic quack*", successfully brought a libel action against him. The expenses and damages together amounted to $8,000 and virtually ruined Cobbett. He decided to return to England and in 1800 the *Porcupine's Gazette* ceased publication. He made one last despairing effort to launch another paper in New York but this was unsuccessful. Cobbett at last yielded to the advice of his friends and sailed for home with his small family in June 1800.

When Priestley's supporter Thomas Jefferson was elected President in 1800, Priestley felt confident enough to write to his brother-in law, John Wilkinson, of the increasingly favourable turn of events for him in America. He was at last at relative peace and able to devote his last three years more to theology rather than politics.

Cobbett in Britain
On his return to Britain, Cobbett settled for a while in London before moving his family to a farm in Hampshire where he could indulge in one of his principal passions in life, his love of farming.

But he remained a voluminous political writer. In 1802 he launched his famous periodical, the *Political Register*, which made it its business to criticise the government. Although condemned by his opponents as *"two penny trash"*, the *Register* was published virtually every week from 1802 until Cobbett's death in 1835. By speaking in language that they could identify with and understand, it had an enormous influence on rousing the working people of Britain to demand reform.

He was always at his best when condemning corruption and specific abuses. In 1810, he went to prison for two years after denouncing the flogging of soldiers who had protested against unfair deductions from their pay.

By 1817 the threat of arrest and money problems sent him back to America where he farmed for a short time in Long Island. On his return to England in 1819, he brought back with him the bones of Thomas Paine who had been laid to rest in America some ten years earlier. Since Cobbett had little time for Paine, once describing him as, *"an unconscionable dog"*, this seems to have been a rather facetious gesture on his part. Apparently, on landing in Liverpool, he soon left the bones to take care of themselves.

During the 1820s and 30s, Cobbett defended several popular causes but none greater than his efforts to speak and act for the agrarian workers of Britain, especially those in the southern counties of England. He was a country man through and through, who profoundly disliked the impact of the Industrial Revolution on society and the environment. He characterised London as the *"Great Wen"* for consuming most of the produce of the countryside and imposing taxes that deprived rural workers of their traditional fare of bread, bacon and beer.

His famous *Rural Rides* conducted between 1821 and 1826 convinced him that agricultural workers were barely subsisting. He warned the government of the coming of a major rural revolt, a prediction borne out in 1830–31 when rural workers in the southern counties rebelled during the so-called *Captain Swing* disturbances. Lord Grey's government suspected that Cobbett was implicated in the revolt and put him on trial, but he was acquitted when the jury was unable to agree on a verdict.

Cobbett's campaign for Parliamentary reform came to fruition when the Reform Act was passed in 1832 and he became a member of parliament for the new parliamentary borough of Oldham. He continued to work for the interests of agricultural workers but the routine and rowdiness of Parliament did not suit him. He was used to being listened to with respect at meetings, but he was now faced with clamour and jeering which he likened to "*the noise of a pack of dogs howling at the moon*".[22]

50. Cobbett as an MP

Sadly, his final years were not happy ones. Never an easy man to live with, he had unhappy conflicts with his wife Anne and family, and suffered something of a persecution complex. He rented a farm close to his birthplace in Farnham. It was there, five days after writing his last article for the *Register*, that this great but headstrong and impetuous man died in June 1835. He was buried in pouring rain beside his father in St Andrew's churchyard, Farnham, leaving a bankrupt estate. It was reported that 8,000 people attended his funeral.

Conclusion

Joseph Priestley was unlucky that, when he left England for America in 1794, it was William Cobbett who should be lying in wait for him. In Priestley, the young Cobbett found just the target he was looking for. The Doctor's political and religious activities made him an obvious target for Cobbett – the near perfect *Aunt Sally*. The cruel and abusive attacks inflicted by Cobbett on Priestley, even for the standards of the time, were little short of outrageous. However, his denunciation of Priestley was historically important as it launched Cobbett on a career that was to make him a major political writer and a popular hero of his age.

Priestley was a resilient man and not one to shun controversy, but in Cobbett he came up against someone who was very different from others with whom he had crossed swords. Priestley flourished in the world of intellect, doctrine and scholarship. Cobbett, on the other hand, was not a theorist, but a practical man driven by his emotions who had little interest in indulging in ideas for the sake of them. He instinctively distrusted any new order based on abstract concepts. Unlike Priestley, he was not inspired by the Enlightenment, and certainly not by the French Revolution with its ideals of Liberty, Equality and Fraternity. He loved nothing better than a good, hot polemical set-to. He could be brutal and even he confessed that *"I may have laid on the lash without regard to mercy"*. But he could write with boldness, originality, passion and humour which much appealed to his public. Even if Priestley had decided to respond fully to all of Cobbett's tirades, it is very likely that Priestley would have come off the worse.

CHAPTER 12

The Presidents: George Washington, John Adams and Thomas Jefferson
Changes of Fortune

Joseph Priestley spent the last ten years of his life living in the United States at a pivotal time in American history. He was well-known to the first three Presidents of the United States – George Washington, John Adams and Thomas Jefferson. His friendship with Washington was amiable and respectful but restrained. His relationship with Adams began auspiciously but was eventually fractured by political differences arising during Adams's presidency. He was closest of all to Jefferson with whom he forged a happy and rewarding partnership in the last few years of his life.

George Washington
George Washington was the first President of the United States and is generally recognised as its *"Founding Father"*. It was largely through his leadership that the Thirteen Colonies became the United States, a sovereign and independent republic. Although a strong willed man with a fiery temper, he nonetheless strove to hold it in check by constant self-discipline, patience, moderation and respect for others both high and low. When he died Congress passed a resolution extolling him as *"First in war, first in peace, and first in the hearts of his countrymen"*.

The First President's Life
Washington was born into a well-off farming family in Wakefield, Virginia in 1732. Little is known of his early life. His education was rudimentary but he soon revealed an aptitude for mathematics. By the age of 15 he was competent as a field surveyor and expert in the practical ways of exploring and living in the wilderness. His skills were recognised by the British, and in 1753 he began his military career when he was appointed as a major in the British Army. At the time, Britain and France were enemies, and Washington led a force to challenge the French control of the Ohio River valley. However he met defeat at Fort Necessity, an event that helped trigger the French and Indian War of 1754–63. Promoted to colonel, he continued to serve bravely in the Army. Irritated by

what he felt to be the lack of respect shown to him and his Virginia militia, Washington resigned his commission and returned to manage his plantations in Virginia.

In 1759, he married Martha Custis, a wealthy widow and mother of two children. He became a member of the Virginia House of Burgesses by 1770 and was one of the first prominent Americans to support open resistance to the taxation and regulation policies imposed by Britain on the colonies in the early 1770s. He represented Virginia at the First and Second Continental Congresses, and in 1775 after the first two military battles of the Revolutionary war at Lexington and Concord, the Congress appointed him Commander-in-Chief of the all the colonial forces in the war with Britain.

Serving without pay, Washington had to overcome severe obstacles especially in the supply of materials and holding together a disciplined army. Over the next five years he manoeuvred his forces superbly and succeeded in harassing the British and avoiding pitched battles. In 1778, the French agreed an alliance with the Americans which marked a turning point in the war. In October 1781, Washington's troops, assisted by the French navy, defeated the British under General Cornwallis at Yorktown and, by the following spring, hostilities between the two countries ended.

After the war, Washington resisted proposals that the military should take over the government and that he should even be appointed as King. He never

51. George Washington

52. Washington resigns his commission as Commander-in-Chief on 23 December 1783

coveted power. He resigned his post as Commander-in-Chief of the army and returned to farm his tobacco plantations. However he was persuaded by his friends to preside over the Constitutional Convention of 1787. Following ratification of the new instruments of government in 1788, he was unanimously chosen by the new Electoral College to be the first President of the Republic of the United States.

Washington served two terms of office from 1789 to 1797. He believed firmly in the need for a strong but cautious central authority and struggled to prevent the emergence of political parties, believing that they would become fractious, self-serving and harmful to the public good. He insisted on his power to act independently of Congress in foreign affairs and, when war broke out between Britain and France in 1795, he personally issued America's Declaration of Neutrality. He was keenly aware that his Presidency would lay down precedents for future administrations and it was largely during his term of office that the country's major government institutions, its offices of state and important constitutional practices were secured.

Weary of politics, he refused to heed the wishes of many people that he should serve a third term. In his farewell address of 1796, he urged his countrymen to renounce party politics and to avoid becoming entangled in wars and the domestic affairs of other countries. He enjoyed only a few years' retirement at his home at Mount Vernon and died at the age of 67 in 1799. In his will, he emancipated all his slaves.

53. Arriving for dinner at Mount Vernon, Washington's home

Washington and Priestley

George Washington and Joseph Priestley could not be described as intimate friends since their paths crossed in America only during the last few years of their lives. The relationship between the two men was restrained compared with Priestley's connection with John Adams and Thomas Jefferson. However, there was considerable respect and admiration between Washington and Priestley for their respective courage and achievements.

Washington was well aware of Priestley's fame as a scientist and theologian and, along with Jefferson and Adams, was quick to send a letter of welcome to Priestley and his family when they arrived in Philadelphia in 1794. Priestley was soon honoured by being formally received by the President. Washington had a rather remote and austere personality and he and his wife normally treated visitors with stiff formality. But the meeting with Priestley turned out to be a warm and friendly occasion and Priestley received an invitation to "*come at any time without authority*". Thereafter, whenever Priestley was in Philadelphia, he and the President would try to meet, and were said to enjoy many hours of sociable conversation.[1]

Intellectually, their interests differed. More a doer than a thinker, Washington had lived such an active life that he never acquired the same familiarity with religion, philosophy and science as Priestley. Nevertheless, he was familiar with Priestley's writings and made a point of keeping his books in his library along with those of Francois-Marie Voltaire and Thomas Paine. Priestley, in return, much admired the moral stature of the President, his firm belief in the duty of those in power to work for the good of their country, and the self-sacrifices he had made in the struggle for American independence. He was impressed too by the President's resistance to popular sentiment urging him to be given more powers and to be treated as something of a king; he approved too of the steps Washington took to avoid the pomp and ceremony of European royal courts.

However, they had their differences. Priestley, for example, was critical of some of the President's political acts, such as his use for the first time in 1794 of federal troops to quell the so-called Whiskey Rebellion in Pennsylvania, and the support he gave for the Alien and Sedition Acts passed later by the Adams administration in 1798. Their attitude towards religion was clearly very different. To Priestley, religion was the *"great business of life"*, and he was adamant that theological enquiry and discussion were superior to all other subjects. Washington, on the other hand, was always reticent about disclosing his personal religious feelings, which has left countless historians and biographers differing as to whether or not he was indeed actually a Christian. Although baptised in the Church of England, he was not a pious man and rarely attended church and never took Holy Communion. The consensus of opinion seems to be that Washington was more a deist than a Christian. The Church undoubtedly had its place in his thinking, but he never allowed it to influence his emotions or affect his political judgement. During his Presidency, Washington rigorously defended the constitutional separation of Church and State in America which was formally recognised in 1791 as part of the First Amendment; this was a stance that would have warmly met with Priestley's approval.

For Priestley and his family, knowing that they were highly regarded by President Washington, and had friendly access to him, meant much to them in their difficult early years in America.

John Adams
John Adams was another highly important leader of the American Revolution. He became the first Vice-President and the second President of the United States. He was a diplomat and political theorist who played a major part in shaping and defending the American constitution. Fiercely independent, he belonged to no particular political party and once wrote that *"I am determined to support every administration whenever I think them in the right"*. Adams was a man of many contrasts and not easy to know. Benjamin Franklin accurately summed him up as a man who *"means well for his country, is always an honest man, often a wise man, but sometimes, and in some things, absolutely out of his senses"*.[2]

Unfortunately Adams's reputation has been overshadowed by his famous contemporaries, such as Washington, Thomas Jefferson and Benjamin Franklin; only relatively recently have Adams's biographers acknowledged the significant contribution he made to the creation and progress of the new Republic in its early days. The Unitarian scholar, Theodore Parker, maintained that, with the exception of Franklin, *"no American politician of the eighteenth*

54. John Adams

century was Adams's intellectual superior", and others have judged that he stands as one of the half-dozen greatest men in American history.[3] His major problem seems to have been his personality; he simply lacked charisma and popular appeal during his own lifetime. Adams recognised his predicament, even to the point of feeling persecuted. *"How is it"*, he complained to his friend Benjamin Rush, *"that I, poor ignorant I, must stand before Posterity as differing from all the other great Men of the Age?"*. He then went on to list those *"greats"* like Joseph Priestley, Benjamin Franklin, Edmund Burke and Thomas Jefferson, and remarked that, even when his own name was bracketed with them, it was often unjustifiably accompanied by qualifications such as *"[Adams was] the most vain, conceited, impudent, and arrogant Creature in the World"*.[4]

The son of a farmer, he had a taste for strong language and did not mince his words. He could be very stern, irascible and was not one for back-slapping and flattery. He had no small talk and admitted that he could think of nothing to say when men's conversation turned to what he believed to be their favourite subjects, women, horses and dogs.[5] He could be pompous and extremely vindictive towards his opponents, and there were many of them. It was said that he never forgave a slight, and succeeded in alienating many of his powerful contemporaries by his outspoken remarks. He could be contemptuous of the achievements of others, even those as distinguished as Washington and Franklin. When asked about the talents responsible for Washington's fame, he answered promptly, it was his handsome face and tall stature, and the fact that he was Virginian and all *"Virginian geese are swans"*. As for Franklin, Adams felt that he had great genius and originality but was far from being a good legislator and politician, and at the Continental Congress he had sat in silence, *"a great part of the time fast asleep in his chair"*.[6]

However, for all his flaws, Adams does seem to have been an honest, self-effacing and courageous man, and a true American patriot. He dedicated his life to public service and the creation of a viable government for the new Republic. In the Continental Congress he sat on 90 committees and chaired 20 of them. Highly intelligent, philosophical and erudite, he won the respect of his colleagues in Congress for quickly grasping the essence of a problem. He was among the first to recognise that George Washington would be the best choice as Commander-in-Chief, and it was on his recommendation that Thomas Jefferson was given the task of drafting the Declaration of Independence.

The Second President's Life
Born in 1735, John Adams was the eldest son of a Massachusetts farmer and shoemaker called Deacon Adams and his wife Susanna. He was brought up in a strict Calvinist household and his father hoped he would become a minister. But John told his father he would rather farm. At the age of 15, he passed the Harvard entrance examination and it was there that he developed a love of learning. He spent a brief period as a teacher but then decided to make a career as a lawyer.

In 1764, he married Abigail Smith, nine years his junior. It was a remarkable marriage, as much of the mind as of the heart. Abigail became as politically astute as her husband and remained his closest confidant throughout his career. She was an early advocate of women's rights.

Adams worked conscientiously at the law, and as his reputation and confidence grew, he became more politically active. He joined with others in opposing taxes which the British Crown had levied on the American colonies to pay for the French and Indian War. Throughout the struggle for independence he worked hard for the cause against the British but stuck to his principles. Always opposed to injustice and mob rule, he courageously and successfully defended eight British soldiers accused of murder in the Boston Massacre.

In 1774, Massachusetts chose Adams to represent the State in the first Continental Congress. He worked obsessively hard and his fluency and mastery of detail meant, rather to his surprise, that he emerged as a natural leader particularly among those who hankered after full independence. It was Adams who proposed the Declaration of Independence in 1775 and he was a member of the committee that finally approved Jefferson's draft. By now he had embraced republicanism. He opposed any semblance of monarchy and aristocratic rule, but acknowledged the need for firm government playing an essential role in the affairs of the nation.

Adams left Congress in 1777 and spent most of the post-Independence years abroad in France, Holland and England on various diplomatic and commercial missions for the new Republic. In May 1785, he became the first United States minister to Great Britain, and in the following year he and Joseph Priestley first met in London. Whilst in England, Adams wrote his massive *Defense of the Constitutions of Government of the United States of America* (1787) which contained much of his political philosophy.

Adam's Calvinism, and his political experience, conspired to give him an increasingly pessimistic view of human nature. He became suspicious of equality and democratic ideals. His fear was that America might well become too much of a democracy and run the risk of deteriorating into tyranny and chaos. Therefore, in his view, it was imperative that safeguards needed to be built into the American constitution. He favoured having three separate branches of government, with the executive branch strong enough to be the *"father and protector"* of the nation. Furthermore, his ideal chief executive needed to be *"more wise, more learn'd, more just, more every thing"* than any other officer of state.[7] These views were strongly reflected in the new Constitution for the United States which was drawn up in Philadelphia later in 1787.

He returned home in 1788 and settled with Abigail on a farm in Braintree, Massachusetts. At first, he wanted to retire from public life but was persuaded to accept the Vice-Presidency in George Washington's administration. Although in practice he had little authority, he loyally supported Washington's

55. Abigail Adams, First Lady, and one of the most influential women of her day

policies, including the rapprochement with Great Britain. However, he became increasingly alarmed by the emergence of partisan politics which seemed to confirm his fear that too much democratisation was indeed driving the new Republic down the path to the same bloodthirsty events that had occurred in France. When Washington announced that he would not stand for a third term, Adams was determined to succeed him. Thomas Jefferson, who was by now his main political rival, also decided to stand for election. By a very close margin Adams defeated him in 1797 and was inaugurated as America's second President.

Early in Adams's administration, America became embroiled with what became known as the "*Quasi-War Crisis*" with France who, since the Jay Treaty of 1794, had announced that trade between the United States and Great Britain would not be tolerated. Relations between America and France degenerated to the point of outright war following the capture of 300 American ships by French privateers claiming that their cargo was British war material. In fact between 1798 and 1800, the United States and France fought a limited but undeclared war.

However, Adams knew that the American Republic was unprepared for a major war and resisted calls from the extreme Federalists in his party to silence the French forever, whom they branded as "*factious, cutthroat, frog-eating, treaty-breaking, grace-fallen, God-defying devils*".[8] In 1800, he decided to settle the crisis by concluding a Convention with France which was secretly negotiated by his son, John Quincy Adams. Nonetheless, during the intervening years, rampant fears of French espionage and revolutionary activity in America formed the background to the infamous Alien and Sedition Acts passed by Adams in 1798, and described later in this chapter.

Partly as a result of his unpopular war measures, Adams lost his bid for a second term in the fierce presidential election battle with Jefferson of 1800. He sold his property to his son John Quincy Adams and retired to his beloved home, Peacefield, in 1801.

At first he was bitter about his election defeat. Piqued by Jefferson's popularity, he lamented that "*I am buried and forgotten*", and despaired that far from heralding a bright new age, the American Revolution had ushered in an "*age of Folly, Vice, Frenzy, Fury, Brutality, Daemons*".[9] Later, however, in the company of his family and his books, he mellowed. After the conclusion of the War with Britain of 1812, America's independence seemed secure, and Adams came to accept that the Revolution had indeed succeeded. In retrospect, he was proud of the major contribution he had made to it, and of the political success of his son, John Quincy Adams, in becoming President in 1824. And to their mutual satisfaction, he and Jefferson became reconciled and corresponded on many topics, especially philosophy and religion. On Independence Day, 4 July 1826,

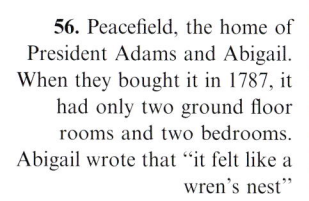

56. Peacefield, the home of President Adams and Abigail. When they bought it in 1787, it had only two ground floor rooms and two bedrooms. Abigail wrote that "it felt like a wren's nest"

both men died within a few hours of one another, said to be *"a coincidence so striking that many contemporaries saw the hand of God in the occurrence"*.[10]

Adams and Priestley

Adams and Priestley had a complicated relationship. They knew one another well and had many interests in common. Adams jotted down in his diary the date – 10 April 1786 – when he first met Priestley in a London bookshop. Adams was aware of Priestley's scientific reputation but it was his religious ideas that interested Adams most, and the following Sunday he went to hear Priestley preach in the Unitarian chapel in Essex Street. The two men quickly became companions and Priestley would have introduced him to several other prominent Unitarians such as Theophilus Lindsey, Richard Price and Thomas Belsham. Over the next few years whilst Adams was ambassador to Britain, he and his wife Abigail regularly attended chapel services conducted by Unitarian preachers, and particularly by Price. Adams later freely admitted that this group of men were in fact his closest friends whilst he was in England.[11]

On Adams's return to the United States, he kept in touch with Priestley and wrote to him in 1792 to express his condolences over the suffering the scientist had endured in the Birmingham riots. When Priestley and his family arrived in America in 1794, Adams urged them to settle near to him in Philadelphia. Priestley did not follow the advice, preferring instead to settle in Northumberland, well over a hundred miles from Philadelphia, but since he occasionally attended and preached at the Unitarian Chapel located there, he was soon able to renew his contact with Adams.

Early in 1796, Adams made a point of attending regularly a series of lectures Priestley gave in Philadelphia on the *Evidence of Revealed Religion*. These lectures were later printed in 1797 with a long dedication from Priestley to Adams who had just become the President. Priestley referred to *"the happiness I have had of your acquaintance and correspondence since your embassy in England ... [and] your steady attachment to the cause of Christianity, the favourable attention you gave to the following Discourses ... and the wish you expressed that they might be published, induce me to take the liberty to dedicate them to you"*.[12] It seems likely that the President would have had mixed feelings about receiving such an effusive dedication; it was about this time that the friendship between the two men had become distinctly cooler and indeed was heading for a complete estrangement.

At the heart of the trouble was America's simmering conflict with France and the increasing animosity in Federalist circles towards all French sympathisers, and especially radical immigrants like Priestley who made no secret of their enthusiasm for the French Revolution and its ideals. A breakfast meeting that Priestley and Adams had together in 1797 betrays the differences that had grown up between the two men. The *"Reign of Terror"* in France had left the President completely disillusioned with the French Revolution, and he asked Priestley if, in his opinion, the French would ultimately establish a Republican Government. Without hesitation Priestley answered, *"that it would"* and, according to Adams, was very eloquent on the subject and declared the Revolution to be *"opening a new era in the world and presenting a near view of the millennium"*.[13] Such a degree of enthusiasm and confidence in the future was hardly shared by a man who by now held a sorry opinion of human nature and of the progress of mankind. In essence, Adams had come to believe that inequality in society was inevitable and that men were just as likely to commit evil as good.

In what seems to have been a calculated snub to Priestley, Adams sought to distance himself from him by taking a Presbyterian pew in Philadelphia rather than attend the Unitarian congregation founded there by the admirers of Priestley. Priestley was clearly disappointed but reflected philosophically *"That any statesman should risk his popularity on account of religion is not to be expected. He would have been the first in any similar situation if he had done it. I suppose too, he was not pleased that I did not adopt his dislike of the French"*.[14]

Relations between Priestley and Adams deteriorated further into a complete breach as political tensions in America worsened in the light of the war crisis with France. Anti-French mania grew, and there was fierce pressure on the government from the Federalist party to protect the country from its domestic enemies, and especially immigrants. Priestley's French and revolutionary sympathies made him a prominent target for public attack, not least by the virulent propagandist, William Cobbett, who had no hesitation in branding Priestley as a French spy (Chapter 11). Under public and political pressure, Adams's administration was forced into action, and its response took the form of the Alien and Sedition Laws of 1798.

The Alien and Sedition Acts
The Alien and Sedition Acts have been called the *"biggest blunder of Adams's blunder-prone administration"*.[15] In fairness to the President, he went to his grave asserting that he never supported these statutes, but he did nevertheless sign them, and they probably eventually cost him the presidential election of 1800.

The Acts comprised three measures. The Alien Friends Act applied generally to all foreign-born residents living in the United States, especially those who were pro-French and very likely to support the Republican Democratic party. Within a two year period, foreigners could be deported or silenced under this Act without the right of redress or appeal. Another Act, the Alien Enemies Act, provided more stringent measures for use in case of war. Because the stand-off between America and France did not escalate into war, it was only the Alien Friends Act that could be used against foreigners. The Sedition Act was passed to deal with domestic, that is American, critics of the government who published *"any false, scandalous and malicious writings – with intent to defame the said government, or either house of the said Congress, or the said President"*. Since the distinction between the Acts was not always clearly drawn, it was often not obvious which law was being applied to individual cases.

Given Priestley's sympathies and radical reputation, the legislation certainly spelt trouble for him. When he had first arrived in America, Priestley had written that he *"made it a rule to take no part whatever in the politics of a country in which I am a stranger"*.[16] Soon after the Alien Acts had been passed he declared again that he had no interest in politics saying, *"I only read the Newspapers once a week, and seldom anything more than the articles of news"*.[17]

Despite these good intentions, it was predictable that someone with his deeply held radical views and interests would get drawn into American politics, and unfortunately this was exactly what happened. However, since he was not an American citizen, he could only be prosecuted under the Alien Laws. On the other hand his firebrand of a friend, Thomas Cooper, had become an American citizen, and he was successfully prosecuted under the Sedition Act for some scathing attacks he had made on Adams in the *Northumberland Gazette* in June 1799 (Chapter 9).

Very soon the focus of attention turned to Priestley who, it was rumoured, had been involved in getting Cooper's article printed and distributed. This was reported to the Secretary of State, Timothy Pickering, who took his responsibility for enforcing the new legislation very seriously. He notified the President about the allegations against Priestley, and remonstrated about *"the Doctor's lack of decency"* and *"his discontented and turbulent spirit, that will never be* quiet under the freest government on earth".[18] Pickering was probably confident that Adams would agree to have Priestley removed from the United States in order to maintain "*our internal tranquillity*", but the President would have none of it. In the same letter in which he authorised the use of the Sedition Act against Cooper, he notified Pickering that "*I do think it wise to execute the Alien Act against poor Priestley at present. He is as weak as water, as unstable as Reuben, or the wind. His influence is not an atom in the world*".[19] Nonetheless, President Adams realised that his erstwhile friend could be his own worst enemy and privately urged him to remain quiet.

Unfortunately, remaining quiet was not in Priestley's nature. In the summer of 1799, Priestley openly attended meetings in Northumberland at which "*democratic*" toasts were drunk and the Adams administration criticised. In August of that year William Cobbett renewed his attack on Priestley by re-publishing the damaging letters from Hurford Stone to Priestley (Chapter 11) which intensified the danger of Priestley's deportation. Spurning the entreaties of his friends not to react, Priestley decided that he should publicly defend his political opinions. In November 1799, he published his *Letters to the Inhabitants of Northumberland*. Unfortunately, as noted earlier in Chapter 11, the *Letters* at first did him more harm than good. Priestley could not resist defending the French Revolution while deploring its atrocities. He also gave support to Jefferson's campaign for the rights of the various States of the Republic, in contrast to the centralising policies of the Adams administration. Furthermore, Priestley openly condemned the Alien and Sedition Laws as "*Laws calculated to restrain the freedom of speech and of the press ... that I was beyond measure astonished to find them introduced here*". They were, he concluded, designed to keep out of the United States "*the friends of liberty emigrating from Europe, a description of men in which I am proud to rank myself*".[20]

Adams deeply resented Priestley's critical remarks made in the *Letters*, and the fact that his Presidential rival, Jefferson, by praising their content and encouraging their distribution, was able to turn them to his political advantage in the run up to the 1800 election. Nonetheless, Adams, out of respect and loyalty to the memory of his old acquaintance, remained reluctant to move against him. He refused to be a rubber stamp for the extremists in his cabinet like Pickering (whom he dismissed in 1800) and resolutely retained the power of final decision on enforcement. Although some 25 persons were arrested under the Sedition Act and ten convicted, in fact there was not a single act of deportation under the Alien Friends Act which was eventually allowed to expire in June 1800. One of Adams's last acts as President was to appoint John Marshall, an opponent of the Sedition Act, as Chief Justice of the Supreme Court.

In 1801, shortly after Jefferson had become President, Priestley published a second edition of the *Letters* in which he openly referred in the Preface to the fact that he had been told that they had "*contributed something*" to the victory of Jefferson over Adams. However, remarkably, Adams does not seem to have borne any lasting enmity towards his former friend. During his retirement, he made a special study of Priestley's works, and confided to Jefferson that if Priestley had lived he should certainly have corresponded with him. Indeed he was, he said, *"ready to forgive Priestley entirely even though he had great complaints against him for personal injuries and persecutions"*. He even prayed that Priestley *"may be pardoned for it all above"*.[21] And in 1813, he wrote *"I never recollect Dr Priestley, but with tenderness of Sentiment. Certainly one of the greatest Men in the World"*, but he could not resist adding *"and certainly one of the weakest"*.[22]

Thomas Jefferson

Thomas Jefferson, the third President of the United States, is one of the most famous and revered figures in American history. As another of the nation's founding fathers and the principal author of the Declaration of Independence, he helped establish the principles upon which democracy was established and developed in the New World and elsewhere. His interests, abilities and achievements would be extraordinary in any age. He founded a great political party, created a university, invented innumerable machines and gadgets and doubled the territory of the United States. He even undertook to revise the Gospels and to combine the four into one continuous version.

The Third President's Life

Born in 1743 in Albemarle County, Virginia, he was the eldest son of a wealthy plantation owner and at the age of 14 he inherited some 5,000 acres of land and

57. Thomas Jefferson

dozens of slaves. He studied mathematics, history and philosophy at the College of William and Mary in Williamsburg, and later law, under the well-respected lawyer George Wythe who introduced him to many members of Virginia's government. In 1767, Jefferson was admitted to the Virginia Bar and started a successful legal practice. Two years later, he was elected to Virginia's House of Burgesses and soon established himself as a powerful political writer, though he did not impress as an orator. In 1772 he married Martha Skelton, a wealthy widow and they began life together in his partly constructed mountaintop home, *Monticello*. They had six children in ten years, but only two survived infancy. Martha died in 1782, at the age of 34, after what Jefferson described as ten years of *"unbridled happiness"*. He never remarried.

After serving the Continental Congress, during which he drafted the Declaration of Independence, Jefferson returned to his seat in the Virginia state legislature. In 1779, he became the governor of his home state during the War of Independence. He was unfairly blamed for fleeing in the face of a British attack on the State and the charge of cowardice would be used against him later by his political opponents.

In 1784, Congress sent Jefferson to Paris as the United States diplomatic minister to France where he witnessed the events leading up to the French Revolution. He supported the democratic aims of the Revolution although later became repulsed by the bloodshed. On a mission to Britain he was snubbed by King George III and his ministers, an event that confirmed his life-long belief that Britain was America's natural enemy.

He returned to America in 1789 to become the country's first Secretary of State under George Washington, but his sympathy for the revolutionary cause in France and his opposition to the centralising policies of members of Washington's cabinet, especially those of the Treasury Secretary, Alexander Hamilton, led him to resign his position in 1793. In the following years Jefferson gradually emerged as the natural leader of the Democratic Republican Party in their struggle with the Federalists.

He was a reluctant candidate in the 1796 Presidential election but came within three votes of election. Due to a flaw in the Constitution, he assumed the post of Vice-President but remained an opponent of President Adams and the Federalists. In the 1800 election Jefferson defeated Adams and one of his first acts as President was to free everyone who had been jailed under the Alien and Sedition Acts.

Simplicity and informality were the hallmark of his administration and he set about reducing taxes and cutting military expenditure. Major events during his Presidency included war with Tripoli over the Barbary pirates who were harassing American ships (1801–04), the Purchase of the Louisiana territory from France (1803) and the Lewis and Clarke Expedition across America

58. The Louisiana Purchase – Jefferson's Presidential Legacy

(1804–06). He was elected again in 1804 but his second term was troubled by the war between Britain and France both of whom repeatedly violated American sovereignty. In an effort to keep America out of any hostilities, Jefferson persuaded Congress to pass the Embargo Act of 1807 which prohibited the shipping of American products to other nations. The Act was a failure and very unpopular with American businessmen; it was was effectively withdrawn by the end of Jefferson's administration.

After Jefferson retired from office in 1809, he spent his retirement at his *Monticello* home. He devoted his time to managing his estate, entertaining visitors, creating a magnificent library and applying himself to his intellectual interests. He worked on his grand design for the new University of Virginia which was chartered in 1819. He was a great letter writer and entered upon the famous 14 year long correspondence with his former political rival John Adams. He died on 4 July 1826 and was buried at *Monticello*.

There is much to admire in the character of Thomas Jefferson and the multiplicity of his interests. As one of the principal founders of the Republic, he brought wisdom, integrity and foresight to all the great offices of state he held. Unlike Adams, he was an optimist as regards human nature. He was an able philosopher and theorist and in countless letters, essays and addresses, he eloquently expressed his ideals about democracy, freedom and the progress of humanity which have inspired the world ever since. But there is also a less attractive side to his character. Some recent biographies have noted that, despite his forthright words about equality and the abolition of slavery, he remained himself a life-long slaveholder. Almost certainly, he was the father of one or more sons by his household slave, Sally Hemings. Also, Jefferson had been quick to express liberal outrage during Adams's presidency at Federalist

59. Monticello, the home of President Jefferson. He began its design and construction when he was aged 26. It accurately reflects his great creativity and his talents

attempts to suppress Republican editors, but when in 1803 he faced similar criticism, he did not hesitate to suggest that *"a few prosecutions of the most prominent offenders would have a most wholesome effect in restoring the integrity of the presses"*.[23] As far as foreign affairs were concerned, he remained an implacable foe of Great Britain when a more balanced approach was called for.

Jefferson and Priestley
Although Jefferson, during his time in France and visits to England during the 1780s, would have met several of Priestley's friends and acquaintances, the evidence suggests that the first actual meeting between the two men took place in 1797 in Philadelphia when Jefferson attended a series of lectures given by Priestley. However, their philosophical and intellectual ties had been forged well before that date and Priestley had already become something of a mentor to the future president. The two men had exchanged many letters and Jefferson eagerly sought, and carefully studied, Priestley's views on religion, politics and education. He once told Priestley that *"Yours is one of the few lives precious to mankind"*.[24]

As regards Jefferson's religious beliefs, he had been brought up in the Church of England. However, as a student at the William and Mary College, his introduction to the Scottish moral philosophers and other authors of church history had raised serious doubts in his mind about established religious institutions and beliefs. He was greatly impressed by Priestley's publication in 1782, *Corruptions of Christianity*, which contended that the teachings of Jesus and his human character had been obscured and obfuscated in the early Christian centuries, and which argued for a reformed Christian faith. Jefferson accepted this proposition and came to reject the doctrine of the Trinity, Mary's Immaculate Conception and Jesus's miraculous powers, and indeed any other religious opinion or doctrine that seemed to him contrary to natural reason. In 1803, he sent a copy of Priestley's *Corruptions* to his daughter Martha to read *"because it establishes the groundwork of my view on this subject"*.[25] However, much as Jefferson sympathised with Priestley's Unitarian views, and on occasion attended Unitarian services whilst visiting Priestley, he never joined a Unitarian church.

His ideal was a religion unhampered by dogma and priesthood and one which produced the greatest social utility. He would have been familiar with Priestley's opinions on the disestablishment of the Church of England and, as early as 1786, he helped draft Virginia's statute of religious freedom which embodied the freedom of conscience and the principle of the separation of church and state. The statute has become an inspiration for those fighting for religious freedom throughout the world. However, Jefferson's religious attitude incurred the wrath of the established clergy and, like Priestley, he was attacked from the pulpit, and in print by the Federalist pamphleteers, as nothing more than an atheist and an infidel.

Since both men held an optimistic view of human nature and endeavour – the *"indefinite perfectibility of man"* – it was natural that both should see education as extremely important. When he was Governor of Virginia, Jefferson had conceived a plan to reform the educational system of Virginia, and in January 1780 he had written a letter to Priestley in England alluding to his plan for a new college of higher education in Virginia. He had first hoped that it would prove possible to utilise the existing, though moribund, William and Mary College for the venture but nothing had come of it due to the war years. However, once he knew that Priestley had settled in America, he turned to Priestley and other eminent men for help in bringing his dream to fruition. He asked Priestley to recommend a course of instruction in the sciences so that the best professors from Europe could be attracted to teach the subjects.

Priestley was pleased to oblige and, as a basis for further discussion between the two men, sent to Jefferson a pamphlet containing *Hints Concerning Public Education* which he had written some time earlier. He suggested a wide-ranging curriculum that would cater both for men preparing for professional duties and for those who needed a more general liberal education. Priestley in fact advised against the use of foreign professors as likely to demand too much deference from the young and to be engrossed too much in pursuit of their own interests. The construction work on what became the University of Virginia at Charlottesville eventually started in 1817 and opened its doors to its first students in 1825. Priestley, had he lived to see it, would have much approved of the wide and liberal fields open for study at the University, justified by Jefferson on the grounds that *"For here we are not afraid to follow truth wherever it may lead"*.[26]

In the field of politics too, Priestley's influence is similarly discernible. The Virginian's political philosophy was based essentially on the same principles expounded by Priestley – the need for limited government, the separation of powers, peace with the world, the inherent equality of mankind and a resolute belief in the human capacity for self improvement and progress. He found Priestley's *Letters to the Inhabitants of Northumberland* discussed earlier in this chapter particularly welcome because they eloquently expressed his own political views at a crucial time in the run up to the 1800 presidential election. He wrote to Priestley congratulating him on the *Letters*, "*You will know what I thought of them by having sent a dozen sets to Virginia to distribute among my friends*", and "*From the Porcupines of our country you will receive no thanks; but the great mass of our nation will edify and thank you*".[27]

Jefferson's electoral victory in 1800 proved to be a most welcome personal blessing for Priestley since it signalled virtually the end of the attacks on him. One of Jefferson's first acts in becoming President was to write a long letter to Priestley condemning "*the bigotry and reaction of the barbarians*" and praising him as "*the great apostle of science and honesty*". He expressed his confidence in the future of the Republic, "*the storm is now subsiding and the horizon becoming serene ... We can no longer say there is nothing new under the sun*".[28] As for Priestley, he was living at last in a country led by a man who wholeheartedly shared his political philosophy and his optimism in human progress. He responded to Jefferson in congratulating him on "*the glorious reverse that has taken place and which has secured your election. This I flatter myself will be the permanent establishment of truly republican principles in this country, and also contribute to the same desirable event in more distant ones*".[29]

The new President quickly proved to be a calming influence on the political scene, and Priestley soon felt able to write thankfully to friends that "*party-spirit is not so high as it was, owing to the moderation and prudence of Mr Jefferson*", and that, "*To me, the administration of Mr Jefferson is the cause of peculiar satisfaction, as I now, for the first time in my life (and I shall soon enter my 70th year) find myself in any degree of favour with the governor of the country in which I have lived, and I hope I shall die in the same pleasing situation*".[30]

It was a hope fulfilled, for Priestley died peacefully at his home in Northumberland in February 1804, the year in which Jefferson was re-elected as President.

Conclusion

Given the support and encouragement that Priestley had given the American colonists in their struggle for independence, and the high hopes that he had for the new Republic, it was fitting that the last decade of his life should be spent living there even though it fell short of some of his expectations. There were very few people who had the distinction, as did Priestley, of being so close to America's first three Presidents, its founding fathers. Here were three gifted men, very different in character, who each in their own way made an outstanding contribution to the creation and early development of the Republic.

Of the three Presidents, Priestley's friendship with Jefferson proved to be the most influential and the most productive. But all three men, whilst by no means sharing all his views, were stirred by Priestley as a man and thinker, and each one admired him. Even Adams, who had good reason to resent his erstwhile friend's ill-advised involvement in American party politics, agreed that the world would have been a poorer place without him, and that *"This great, excellent and extraordinary Man, whom I sincerely loved, esteemed and respected, was really a Phenomenon: a Comet in the System, like Voltaire"*.[31]

CHAPTER 13

Conclusion

All the individuals covered in this book were remarkable people and some achieved true greatness. It could be argued that their eventful lives and their association with Joseph Priestley speak for themselves, and little more needs to be said. Each one of the personal studies has thrown some light on the nature of some of the major events and challenges of the age, and how the individuals influenced and responded to them. And the studies too reveal much about Joseph Priestley's own life and his influence. But to complete the picture, are there some general conclusions that can be drawn?

Undeniably, all the friends and foes were extraordinarily interesting personalities who through the force of their characters and achievements stamped their mark on the course of events. They were all present as the European Enlightenment unfolded in the second half of the eighteenth century. For all its faults and errors, they believed that they were living in the greatest of times. All were caught up in that heady mixture of philosophical, scientific and industrial discovery, religious and political reform, controversy, cultural change and indeed violence, characteristic of the age. It was the *Age of Authors*; friends and foes took full advantage of the boom in printing and publishing to promote their work and opinions.

Inevitably, their lives were dominated by the huge changes taking place. All were patriots in their own way, and all experienced the repercussions of four great Revolutions – the American, the French, the Industrial and the Scientific Revolutions. George Washington, John Adams and Thomas Jefferson were all present at the creation of the American Republic. The French Revolution led to Priestley fleeing from his homeland, to the emergence of Edmund Burke's reputation as a foremost political thinker and to the early death of the distinguished scientist Antoine Lavoisier. Anna Barbauld became deeply concerned about the impact of both the French and Industrial Revolutions, and confronted the political and social issues in her essays and poems. John Wilkinson, Priestley's brother-in-law, rose from a small iron master to be the greatest and wealthiest industrialist of his age in the space of 20 years. And William Cobbett spent much of his life championing the rural classes against the changes wrought by the Industrial Revolution.

Friends

It is evident that Joseph Priestley had a great capacity for friendship and it was a quality that meant a great deal to him. In his exile in America it was his friends whom Priestley missed most of all. Those portrayed here are but a few of the very wide circle of acquaintances which he made during his lifetime. They were quite different from one another in many ways, and they would no doubt have objected to being classified as if they were members of a particular group.

On the other hand, there are some common characteristics. It was, at the time, a man's world dominated by male elites, and all those described here were men, with the notable exception of Anna Barbauld. They were enthused with the spirit of optimism released by the Enlightenment. All in varying degrees were liberal in terms of their outlook; they talked and worked for something new and better, a break with the past whether political, religious, social or industrial, and the need to reform national institutions. They had an almost naive belief in human progress. Mankind, they thought, had only to observe natural law to be freed from every antiquated legal shackle, superstition and custom and thus bring about freedom from prejudice and oppression. Price, Lindsey and Priestley eagerly looked forward to the approaching Biblical Millennium when, they believed, Divine intervention would further inspire the transformation of society, together with peace and harmony among the nations of Europe. They were all at odds with the conservatism of established religion and none of the friends was a practising member of the Church of England. However, they by no means all shared Priestley's deep-seated religious faith, and at least three – Benjamin Franklin, Thomas Cooper and Thomas Jefferson – had few religious beliefs at all.

Priestley and his British friends were distinctly unfortunate in their timing. At the end of the eighteenth century, Britain not only had deep social and economic problems at home, but was facing the prospect of revolution at home and invasion from abroad. The mood of the nation changed. The early optimism that the French Revolution had engendered soon relapsed into patriotic conservatism. Priestley and his friends found themselves pressing for change when circumstances conspired to bring their enemies together. In fact, more interested in reform rather than revolution, the former group posed no major threat to the established order or of politicising the masses. Much more dangerous was the rise of the radical political organisations fuelled by extremist writings. This was something the authorities could not ignore or ridicule. The very institutions of State and Church seemed threatened. King George III, his government and conservative supporters responded by crushing the organisations and their means of publicity, and were able to denounce the visions of progress pronounced by Priestley and others as being not only unpatriotic but hopelessly utopian.

With their hopes frustrated, the early idealism of several of Priestley's friends gave way to a sense of disillusionment as events unfolded. Barbauld, Franklin and Cooper were openly much more pessimistic about the future of mankind by the end of their lives. President John Adams, a one time friend of Priestley, but who crossed swords with Priestley later in his life, underwent a similar change in outlook.

Priestley readily acknowledged the debt that he owed to his close friends. He loved to exchange ideas, and to share his beliefs and aspirations with them, and took delight in sharing news of his latest discoveries. He turned to them for practical advice and, importantly, for financial help at critical stages in his career. He admitted to Franklin in 1779 that the "expence (sic) of my experiments is necessarily considerable", and that without the support of his friends he would have desisted altogether.[1] When he moved from Bowood to Birmingham in 1780 his friends in the Lunar Society raised a subscription to fund Priestley's new laboratory and equip it with the latest scientific apparatus. The substantial financial support provided by his brother-in-law, John Wilkinson, for Priestley and members of his family was critical at various times in their lives.

His friends helped in other important ways. Franklin acted as his mentor, and launched his scientific career by encouraging his researches and getting him elected to the Fellowship of the Royal Society. Theophilus Lindsey did what he could to safeguard Priestley from the attacks on his political and religious beliefs, and had good connections who were able to help Priestley with the purchase of valuable books and equipment. It was through Richard Price's auspices that Lord Shelburne engaged Priestley as librarian and tutor to his children, which allowed Priestley the time and resources to make a string of discoveries which ensured his name would ever be remembered in the history of chemistry.

In their turn, Priestley's friends owed much to the help, knowledge and inspiration he so readily gave to them. For some, without Priestley, their lives would probably have been very different indeed. It was Priestley who took the leading role in rescuing Theophilus Lindsey in the dark days after the latter had resigned his parish living in Yorkshire, and who worked with him to set up and promote the success of Britain's first Unitarian Chapel. Richard Price and Priestley made a formidable partnership in their campaigns for liberty and freedom whether it concerned the slave trade or the Test and Corporation Acts, or the cause of the American revolutionaries. Anna Barbauld freely acknowledged that it was Priestley and his wife Mary who inspired and nurtured her literary talents as a young woman. Thomas Cooper learned much from Priestley in his early days as a chemist and as a radical activist, and the two men worked and lived closely together in exile in America. And President Thomas Jefferson was inspired by Priestley on several matters during his lifetime and was very grateful for the support he received from him in the presidential election of 1800.

Foes

Turning to the foes of Priestley, they were a most formidable group of men. In terms of such matters as class, background and careers they had little in common. George III was the Head of State of a rich and powerful empire, and for many years that consummate politician and administrator – William Pitt – was his first Minister. Samuel Horsley and Edmund Burke were, respectively, a High Church bishop and a leading politician. The aristocratic Antoine Lavoisier was a wealthy and gifted scientist. William Cobbett rose from a working class background to be one of the most influential journalists of his age. John Adams, too, came from a modest farming background to become one of the founders of the American Revolution and the second President of the United States.

However, there are some striking similarities. All were able, intensely ambitious men who at one time or another found good reason to oppose Priestley. They were forceful and confident people. There was a worldliness about them which left them with little time or interest in the utopian visions of Priestley and some of his friends. True, they were quite capable of expressing their own views in sweeping and idealistic rhetoric, but they were politically adept and recognised the importance of influence and political manoeuvre in achieving their goals.

In sharp contrast to Priestley and his friends, their innate conservatism left them suspicious of change. Lavoisier was the exception in so far as he saw the need for radical changes in the science of chemistry and initially, at least, supported a degree of political and social reform in France. But others amongst the foes were very cautious about the need for any hasty change and stern opponents of any extremes that might threaten the established order. Cobbett once wrote that, "*It is by attempting to reach the top in a single leap so much misery is caused in the world*", a sentiment with which Horsley, Burke and Pitt would have heartily agreed.

When all the dust had settled, it is interesting to observe how several of Priestley's adversaries found their own fortunes enhanced by their confrontation with him. It was once said that if a clergyman wanted advancement in the Anglican Church of the time, he should pick a fight with Priestley. Horsley seized such an opportunity and, at the end of his long and acrimonious theological controversy with Priestley, he was rewarded with his Bishop's mitre and became a national figure. Burke's *Reflections on the Revolution in France* was partly provoked by the views of Priestley, Price and other radicals, and his work established his international reputation and fame as a conservative thinker. Lavoisier's work on combustion and the subsequent development of his New

Chemistry were inspired by Priestley's experiments with gases in the 1770s. And Cobbett, alias Peter Porcupine, first established his reputation as a radical journalist through his scurrilous attacks on Priestley in America, and went on to fame in Britain as *"the people's tribune"*.

Nor should we overlook the fact that Priestley too could prosper from the clashes he had with his enemies. For example, he emerged from his theological controversy with Bishop Horsley with his reputation enhanced as the acknowledged leader of the Unitarian movement in Britain. And scientifically, although his dispute with Lavoisier over the nature of deplogisticated air was misguided, it nonetheless gave wide recognition and publicity to his important achievement as a discoverer of oxygen.

Priestley

One might conclude therefore that Priestley was nourished by the respect, affection and help of his friends, and yet in some respects stimulated by the clashes with his enemies. What more, then, can Priestley's relationship with his friends and foes tell about his own character?

Both groups of people would have little difficulty in agreeing upon certain characteristics. He was very straightforward and the least secretive of men, even to the point of naivety. One reason why he fell out with Lavoisier was his disapproval of the secretive nature of his fellow scientist. Priestley, on the other hand, was always open about his scientific experiments and preferred to conduct them publicly in the provinces, away from the centres of power. He was an accomplished communicator; in an age of pamphleteering, he was the champion pamphleteer. He left no one in doubt of his opinions and feelings in the cause of truth and liberty. He promoted and defended them vigorously and uncompromisingly, even to the extent of endangering himself and his family. His friends, notably Lindsey, often warned him against writing too much and too recklessly, but his meaning was always clear. His prodigious energy and scholarship, and the range of his abilities, were widely recognised. No one doubted his moral courage however much they disliked him. Unlike some of his enemies, he was far from being an intolerant man; although he believed, for example, that Roman Catholics and Jews were deeply misguided, he insisted that they should have the same rights to emancipation as the Dissenters and practised what he preached. He wrote that on one occasion he had *"dined in company with an eminent popish priest; the evening I spent with philosophers, determined unbelievers; the next morning I breakfasted, at his own request, with a most zealously orthodox clergyman, and the rest of the day I spent with ... men in all respects after my own heart"*. He was invariably upright and honourable in his dealings with other people, even with the most malicious of his adversaries, such as Burke and Cobbett.

It was, however, those very qualities which were often turned against him and exploited by his enemies. Priestley's bold and relentless pursuit of his religious and political convictions left no room for compromise or pragmatism. He could be reckless, even irresponsible. In contrast to close friends like Franklin and Jefferson, he lacked the political skills to achieve his ends, notably the understanding that concession and manoeuvre, perhaps even intrigue, could sometimes accomplish more in the long run. Radical pamphlets could be potent weapons but neither he nor his campaigning friend Price knew how to mobilise the politically uneducated and exploit popular discontent. His political naivety led to his downfall. By escalating his criticisms of King, Church and government in the perilous years following the French Revolution, Priestley not only infuriated his enemies, but lost the support of the upper and middle classes, as well as badly damaging the Dissenters' cause.

Even the free and easy approach Priestley used to tell others about his work could be turned against him. Burke used his formidable rhetorical skills to condemn the publicity Priestley gave to his scientific experiments as being essentially destructive, and little more than mere self-indulgent alchemy. Similarly, allowing himself to be drawn into American politics against the advice of his friends during his exile in America was a bad error of judgement on Priestley's part; it lost him the support of his erstwhile ally President Adams, and he was punished cruelly by Cobbett and other opponents.

It is difficult to escape the conclusion that Priestley was perhaps his own worst enemy and actually enjoyed controversy. He was in effect a disputatious man living in a disputatious age. William Hazlitt, the writer, had no doubt that Priestley had been the best controversialist of the day. Apart from his conflict with Lavoisier over the discovery of oxygen, virtually all the major struggles he experienced during his lifetime were dominated by religion and politics and, more often than not, it was he who made the running. He asked for no quarter and gave none. He derived as much satisfaction from refuting the argument of an opponent, or exposing a fallacy, as he did from making a new discovery. As often the case with political and religious controversies, it was often difficult to discern what had been achieved. There is some truth in the observation of Samuel Johnson (another opponent of Priestley) that Priestley tended *"to unsettle everything, and yet settle nothing"*.

However, it has to be said that Priestley was not drawn to controversy for any personal consideration but by his belief that some fundamental aspect of freedom or liberty was at stake. He was convinced that the adversarial approach was the best means of arriving at the truth, and in the tradition of the day it was fair game to make good use of sarcasm, irony and other rhetorical devices.

The book has also revealed the die-hard and stubborn side to Priestley's character. His dispute with Lavoisier over the precedence to the discovery of oxygen, and his dogged adherence to the phlogiston theory are the most striking examples. Even when virtually all the scientific world had been converted to Lavoisier's New Chemistry, he defended resolutely to his dying day the phlogiston theory and insisted that the new science was wrong. There is a parallel too with Priestley's attitude towards the Dutch-born British scientist Jan Ingen Housz in the 1780s over the discovery of photosynthesis. Priestley found it difficult to come to terms with the fact that, although his experiments had first shown that plants give off oxygen, it was Housz who demonstrated a better understanding of the actual process and the importance of sunlight. Similarly, he adopted a purblind attitude to the chaos and bloodshed of the French Revolution; as late as 1797 he was assuring President Adams that it was *"opening a new era in the world"*.

There were other aspects too of Priestley's life that played into the hands of his enemies. Priestley enjoyed the company of his intellectual equals and his social mix was narrow in terms of the rest of society. As a leading member of the Rational Dissenters, he had links with most of the reforming movements of the late eighteenth century, including the Whig political elite as personified by Lord Shelburne. Essentially, their values were middle class; the class which Priestley knew and esteemed the most. Consequently, Priestley showed little understanding of the need to mobilise popular support for reform, especially amongst the poorer classes. On the contrary, he took a rather paternalistic view of class relations and stressed the importance of middle-class charity for the poor as a means of encouraging their own ambition. His moral code embraced in fact many of the principles spelt out in Franklin's *Poor Richard's Almanac* – hard work, a well-ordered life and individual self-sufficiency. Fiercely protective of individual rights, Priestley distrusted state action of any kind, including social safety nets such as the Poor Laws, and took the view that *"individuals when left to themselves are, in general, sufficiently provident and will daily better their circumstances"*.[2] Like other Rational Dissenters he held firmly conservative views about the necessity for strong social discipline and authority if the morals of the poor were to be improved, and advocated strong punishment for criminals.

Perhaps, therefore, it is not surprising that with these views Priestley never won the sympathy and confidence of the working class, let alone the 'mob'. Moreover, his controversial religious beliefs, purged of all that he considered irrational, lacked warmth. Coleridge aptly compared the form of Unitarianism that Priestley followed as moonlight – cold and clear. Similarly, Priestley's morality and disciplined life style were simply too distant from the harsh realities of the daily lives of working class people to hold much attraction for them. His friend, Anna Barbauld, showed a greater understanding of ordinary people, and appreciated in her writings why the poet and novelist could have a greater public appeal than the philosopher and scientist, especially at the dawn of a more romantic period. Priestley's enemies spotted his vulnerability and ruthlessly branded him as a gloomy, puritanical man and dangerous fanatic, whose unpopularity among the *'mob'* could be readily exploited, as in the Birmingham riots of 1791. Later in America, Cobbett was another to see that Priestley's apparent lack of humour and strict middle-class morality made him a perfect target for portrayal of him as *"a miserable perverse old man, a perverse hypocrite and an unnatural monster"*.[3]

In fact, as we have seen, Priestley was by no means a gloomy fanatic. He had a kind, cheerful and generous personality and in spite of his bitter enemies, he was far from being uncharitable to his opponents. It is a sad reflection on Priestley's life that those who hated him the most seemed to have known him the least.

America

The American connection has been a prominent theme of this book. It was an American, Benjamin Franklin, in many ways the archetypal Enlightenment man, who had first set Priestley on his path as a great scientist. Priestley, like many others before him, was deeply attracted to the promise of America as being the most enlightened of all nations and *"an asylum for the friends of liberty"*. He had readily admitted, back in 1772 when a minister at Leeds, that if he ever left England it would be for America. He had greeted the American Revolution (and later the French) as confirmation that his millennium beliefs were indeed being borne out.

Priestley's high hopes for America were shared, too, by his friends and compatriots Richard Price and Theophilus Lindsey. Price in particular did much to popularise the dream of America. He had campaigned prominently for the American revolutionaries, and greeted their successful struggle as opening up a new era in the history of mankind. The fledgling Republic later offered American citizenship to Price in gratitude for all the advice and help he had provided for it. Anna Barbauld was another who believed that the future lay with America; in her poem, *Eighteen Hundred and Eleven*, she portrayed Britain in decline and predicted that the future of civilisation would soon pass to America. Thomas Cooper, after finding life in England too dangerous, settled in Pennsylvania near the Priestleys' home. He seems to have recognised more clearly than Priestley the fact that America and England had become two distinct nations, and adopted American citizenship. He later contributed much to the public life of his adopted country.

The American connection too loomed strongly among Priestley's adversaries. The American Revolution dominated British politics in the early years of the reign of George III. Although Pitt wanted the end of the war with the American colonists, the King held to the simple belief that the future of Britain's empire and monarchy was at stake, and that the American revolutionists had to be

60. An early representation of the American Dream depicting America as a Garden of Eden without hatred or war. Painted by the American Quaker, Edward Hicks (1780–1849)

crushed. To him, their supporters like Priestley and Price were nothing less than traitors and he never forgave them. Edmund Burke came into sharp conflict with Priestley on other issues, but the support Burke gave to the American colonists was one of the major convictions of his parliamentary career, and Priestley had admired him for it. William Cobbett sought refuge in America and it was there that he launched his career as radical journalist. As for Antoine Lavoisier, it is claimed he made an important contribution to the decisive British defeat by the American colonists at Yorktown in 1781. During the 1770s he had improved the composition of gunpowder so much so that it could carry a cannon ball very much further than any other powder in Europe, and French gunpowder was shipped in large quantities to America during the War of Independence,

Finally, America was the country in which Joseph Priestley sought sanctuary and which provided him with his final resting place. When President Jefferson took power in 1800, it can be said that Priestley, after all his years of turmoil, had at last found peace under a government sympathetic to his ideals and aspirations. Some 30 years earlier, Theophilus Lindsey, arguably the closest of all Priestley's friends, had recorded that he had dined with the Doctors Price and Priestley, and two Americans – Franklin and the revolutionary patriot, Josiah Quincy. He concluded his account with the comment, *"No bad company, you will say. We began and ended with the Americans"*.[4] Not, perhaps, a bad epitaph on which to close the story of Joseph Priestley's life and those of his friends and foes.

Notes

Chapter 1: Priestley's World
1. Roy Porter, *Enlightenment*, p. 406.
2. Jenny Uglow, *The Lunar Men*.
3. William Blake, quoted in Porter, *op. cit.*, p. 403.
4. Joseph Priestley, quoted in Porter, *op. cit.*, p. 398.
5. Jenny Graham, *Revolutionary in Exile*, p. 164.

Chapter 2: Benjamin Franklin
1. R. Middlekauff, *Benjamin Franklin and his Enemies*, p. 3.
2. Benjamin Franklin, *Poor Richard's Almanac, 1773–1747*.
3. P. Russell, *Benjamin Franklin*, p. 141.
4. Middlekauff, *op. cit.*, p. xvi.
5. *Ibid.*, p. xviii.
6. D. McCullough, *John Adams*, p. 198.
7. Middlekauff, *op. cit.*, p. xix.
8. Priestley, *Autobiography of Joseph Priestley*, p. 117.
9. C. Van Doren, *Benjamin Franklin*, p. 777.
10. http://www.royalsoc.ac.uk./page.asp?tip=1&id=4873.
11. C. Van Doren, *op. cit.*, p. 718.
12. J. Jackson, *A World on Fire*, p. 66.
13. Middlekauff, *op. cit.*, p. 10.
14. Priestley, *op. cit.*, p. 117.
15. J.B. McMaster, *Benjamin Franklin*, p. 222.
16. Benjamin Franklin Papers, *Letter to Priestley*, 7 June 1782.
17. Russell, *op. cit.*, p. 312.
18. *Ibid.*, p. 319.

Chapter 3: Richard Price
1. J.T. Rutt (ed.), *Collected Life and Correspondence of Joseph Priestley*, Vol. 1, p. 23.
2. Priestley, quoted in R. Thomas, *Philosopher and Apostle of Liberty*, p. 149.
3. Howard, quoted in R. Thomas, p. 153.
4. R. Thomas, *op. cit.*, p.151.
5. Price, quoted in D.O. Thomas, *The Honest Mind*, p. 128.
6. C.B. Cone, *Torchbearer of Freedom*, p. 149.
7. J. Jackson, *A World on Fire*, p. 198.
8. Cone, *op. cit.*, p. 79.
9. Rutt, *op. cit.*, Vol. 1, pp. 289–90.
10. Priestley, quoted in D.O. Thomas, *op. cit.*, p. 152.
11. Am. Congress, quoted in D.O. Thomas, *op. cit.*, p. 260.

12. D.O. Thomas, *op. cit.*, p. 262.
13. Price, quoted in D.O. Thomas, *op. cit.*, p. 295.
14. *Ibid.*, pp. 301–2.
15. Burke, quoted at: http://www.100welshheroes.com/en/biography/drrichardprice.
16. Quoted in Cone, *op. cit.*, p. 197.
17. *Ibid.*, p. 200.
18. Priestley, quoted in F.W. Gibbs, *Joseph Priestley*, p. 195.
19. J.D. Bowers, *Joseph Priestley and English Unitarianism in America*, p. 169.

Chapter 4: John Wilkinson
1. N.C. Soldon, *John Wilkinson (1728–1808), English Ironmaster and Inventor*, p. 25.
2. *Ibid.*, p. 124.
3. http://www.broseley.org.uk/wilkfiles/us.htm.
4. Priestley–Wilkinson correspondence, Warrington Public Library.
5. Priestley, quoted in W.H. Chaloner, *Dr Joseph Priestley, John Wilkinson and the French Revolution, 1889–1802*, Trans. Royal Hist. Soc., Vol. 8, pp. 23–4.
6. *Ibid.*, p. 28.
7. Soldon, *op. cit.*, p. 331.
8. R. Davies, *John Wilkinson*, p. 25.

Chapter 5: Anna Barbauld
1. Priestley, *Autobiography*, p. 89.
2. B. Rodgers, *Georgian Chronicle*, p. 83.
3. *Ibid.*, p. 52.
4. Barbauld, poem, quoted in D. Wakefield, *Anna Laetitia Barbauld*, p. 26.
5. D. Coleman, in Russell and Tuite, *Romantic Sensibility*, p. 87.
6. Rodgers, *op. cit.*, p. 61.
7. D. Wakefield, *op. cit.*, p. 31.
8. Lucy Aikin, quoted in Rodgers, *op. cit.*, p. 62.
9. Rodgers, *op. cit.*, p. 63.
10. *Ibid.*, p. 76.
11. *Ibid.*, ref. p. 198.
12. Coleman, *op. cit.*, p. 84.
13. Barbauld, quoted in Coleman, *op. cit.*, p. 88.
14. Rutt, *Theological*, Vol. 2, quoted in Coleman, *op. cit.*, p. 88.
15. Wakefield, *op. cit.*, pp. 35/36.
16. Priestley, quoted in Coleman, *op. cit.*, p. 88.
17. Coleman, *op. cit.*, p. 85.
18. Rodgers, *op. cit.*, p. 71.
19. Rodgers, *op. cit.*, p. 100.
20. Barbauld, Poem, quoted in Coleman, *op. cit.*, p. 100.
21. Wakefield, *op. cit.*, p. 67.
22. Rutt, quoted in Coleman, p. 97.
23. *Ibid.*, p. 98.
24. Rodgers, *op.cit.*, p. 136.
25. Barbauld, poem, quoted in Rodgers, *op. cit.*, p. 140.
26. Quarterly Review, quoted in Rodgers, *op. cit.*, p. 141.
27. Edgeworth, quoted in Rodgers, *op. cit.*, p. 153.

Chapter 6: Theophilus Lindsey

1. G.M. Ditchfield, *Joseph Priestley and Theophilus Lindsey*, Trans. Unitarian Historical Soc., April 2004, p. 496.
2. G.M. Ditchfield, *Theophilus Lindsey: From Anglican to Unitarian*, Lecture to Friends of Dr Williams's Library, October 1997, p. 19.
3. http://en.wikipedia.org/wiki/Joseph_Priestley_and_Dissent, p. 2.
4. Ditchfield, *Joseph Priestley and Theophilus Lindsey*, *op. cit.*, p. 502.
5. Quoted in G.M. Ditchfield, *A Unitarian Saint? Theophilus Lindsey 1723–1808*, p. 81.
6. J. Priestley, *Autobiography*, p. 98.
7. T. Belsham, *Memoirs of Theophilus Lindsey*, p. 143.
8. *Ibid.*, p. 242.
9. *Ibid.*, p. 240.
10. *Ibid.*, p. 287.
11. Ditchfield, *Joseph Priestley and Theophilus Lindsey*, *op. cit.*, p. 509.
12. Belsham, *op. cit.*, p. 312.

Chapter 7: Antoine Lavoisier

1. C. Djerassi and R. Hoffmann, *Oxygen*.
2. S.J. French, *Torch and Crucible: The Life and Death of Antoine Lavoisier*, p. 124.
3. W.R. Aykroyd, *Three Philosophers*, p. 63.
4. http://www.chemheritage.org/classroom/chemach/forerunners/lavoisier.htm.
5. J. Priestley, *The Discovery of Oxygen*, quoted in J. Jackson, *A World on Fire*, p. 172.
6. French, *op. cit.*, p. 86.
7. Jackson, *op. cit.*, p. 151.
8. French, *op. cit.*, p. 88.
9. *Ibid.*, p. 89.
10. *Ibid.*, p. 98.
11. *Ibid.*, pp. 98–9.
12. *Ibid.*, p. 100.
13. http://antoine.frostburg.edu/chem/senese/101/history/faq/discovery-of-oxygen.shtml.
14. Jackson, *op. cit.*, p. 192.
15. *Ibid.*, p. 216.
16. A.J. Berry, *From Classical to Modern Chemistry: Some Historical Sketches*, p. 23.
17. Jackson, *op. cit.*, p. 219.
18. http://www.1911encyclopedia.org/Joseph_Priestley.
19. French, *op. cit.*, p. 255.
20. S.J. Gould, *Bully for Brontosaurus: Reflections in Natural History*, p. 364.
21. http://en.wikipedia.org/wiki/Antoine_Priestley.
22. French, *op. cit.*, p. 214.

Chapter 8: Samuel Horsley

1. F.C. Mather, *High Church Prophet*, Preface.
2. Quote by Lord Keynes, Mather, *op. cit.*, p. 47.
3. http://www.newtonproject.sussex.ac.uk.
4. Mather, *op. cit.*, p. 51.
5. *Ibid.*, p. 54.
6. Horsley, quoted in A.D. Holt, *A life of Joseph Priestley*, p. 135.
7. Mather, *op. cit.*, p. 58
8. F.W. Gibbs, *Joseph Priestley, Adventurer in Science and Champion of Truth*, p. 173.

9. Priestley, quoted in Mather, *op. cit.*, p. 59.
10. Horsley, quoted in Gibbs, *op. cit.*, p. 174.
11. Jebb, quoted in Mather, *op. cit.*, p. 58.
12. Mather, *op. cit.*, p. 59.
13. J.C.D. Clark, *English Society*, p. 232.
14. Clark, *op. cit.*, p. 233.
15. Archbishop Markham, quoted in R.A. Soloway, *Prelates and People, Ecclesiastical Social Thought in England, 1783–1852*, p. 33.
16. Soloway, *op. cit.*, p. 33.
17. Horsley, quoted in Soloway, *op. cit.*, p. 40.
18. http://www.bartleby.com.

Chapter 9: Thomas Cooper
1. Jefferson, quoted in Seymour S. Cohen, *Two Refugee Chemists in the United States: How We See Them*, Proceedings of the Am. Philosophical Soc., Vol. 126, No. 4, August, 1982, p. 302.
2. http://www.nationmaster.com/encyclopedia/Thomas-Cooper.
3. http://www.lycolaw.org/history/sketches/06.htm.
4. Cooper, quoted in Dumas Malone, *The Public Life of Thomas Cooper*, p. 14.
5. Priestley, quoted in Cohen, *op. cit.*, p. 308.
6. Cohen, *op. cit.*, p. 309.
7. Cooper, quoted in Dumas Malone, *op. cit.*, p. 78.
8. J. Graham, *Revolutionary in Exile*, p. 64.
9. *Ibid.*, p. 81.
10. *Ibid.*, p. 82.
11. *Ibid.*, p. 86.
12. *Ibid.*, p. 85.
13. Dumas Malone, *op. cit.*, pp. 17–18.
14. Priestley, quoted in Dumas Malone, *op. cit.*, p. 86.
15. Adams, quoted in Graham, *op. cit.*, p. 123.
16. Thomas Cooper, quoted in DNB, S.L. Newman.
17. http://www.nationmaster.com/encyclopedia/Thomas-Cooper.

Chapter 10: King George III, William Pitt and Edmund Burke
1. Letter from George III to Lord North, in B. Dobree, *The Letters of King George III*, pp. 139–40.
2. Letter from George III to Dundas, in Dobree, *op. cit.*, p. 212.
3. Priestley, Letter to William Pitt, quoted in P. O'Brien, *Debate Aborted 1789–91*, p. 167.
4. F.W. Gibbs, *Joseph Priestley, Adventurer in Science and Champion of Truth*, p. 181.
5. Priestley, quoted in http://www.spartacus.schoolnet.co.uk/PRpriestley.htm.
6. E. Royle and J. Walvin, *English Radicals and Reformers*, p. 55.
7. Quoted in E.P. Thompson, *The Making of the English Working Class*, p. 118.
8. Pitt, quoted in Royle and Walvin, *op. cit.*, p. 60.
9. R.B. Dozier, *For King, Constitution and Country*, p. 157.
10. Pitt, quoted in J. Ehrman, *The Younger Pitt*, p. 829.
11. K. Feiling, *A History of England*, p. 740.
12. A. Cobban, *Edmund Burke and the Revolt against the Eighteenth Century*, p. 76.
13. J. Todd, *Mary Wollstonecraft*, p. 163
14. http://www.en.wikipedia.org/wki/Edmund_Burke.
15. P. O'Brien, *op. cit.*, p. 260.

16. Paine, quoted in Royle and Walvin, *op.cit.*, p. 44.
17. Burke, quoted in *Autobiography of Joseph Priestley*, p. 28.
18. DNB, *King George III*.
19. Priestley, quoted in P.O. O'Brien, *op. cit.*, pp. 41–2.
20. J. Jackson, *A World on Fire*, p. 244.

Chapter 11: William Cobbett
1. Priestley, quoted in J Graham, *Revolutionary in Exile*, p. 50.
2. *American Daily Advertiser*, quoted in L.C. Newell, *Peter Porcupine's Persecution of Priestley*, Journal of Chemical Education, March, 1933, p. 153.
3. *Ibid.*, p. 153.
4. *Ibid.*, p. 154.
5. Graham, *op. cit.*, p. 50.
6. *Ibid.*, p. 54.
7. Cobbett, quoted in E.F. Smith, *Priestley in America*, p. 42.
8. Cobbett, quoted in Newell, *op. cit.*, p. 156.
9. Graham, *op. cit.*, p. 53.
10. Cobbett, quoted in Newell, *op. cit.*, p. 157.
11. *Ibid.*, p. 157.
12. *Ibid.*, p. 159.
13. Smith, *op. cit.*, pp. 43–5.
14. Lewis Melville, *The Life and Letters of William Cobbett*, p. 108.
15. Priestley, quoted in Graham, *op. cit.*, p. 98.
16. Stone, quoted in Graham, *op. cit.*, p. 111.
17. Cobbett, quoted in Graham, *op. cit.*, p. 113.
18. Priestley, quoted in Graham, *op. cit.*, p. 114.
19. Jefferson, quoted in Graham, *op. cit.*, p. 143.
20. G.D.H. Cole, *The Life of William Cobbett*, p. 54.
21. http://www.blupete.com/Literature/Biographies/Philosophy/Cobbett.htm.
22. *Ibid.*

Chapter 12: Presidents George Washington, John Adams and Thomas Jefferson
1. F.W. Gibbs, *Joseph Priestley*, p. 231.
2. Z. Haraszti, *John Adams and the Prophets of Progress*, p. 5.
3. http://www.bbc.co.uk/dna/h2g2/A10083935.
4. J.J. Ellis, *The Passionate Sage: The Character and Legacy of John Adams*, p. 57.
5. J. Ferling, *Adams vs. Jefferson*, p. 22.
6. Adams, quoted in Haraszti, *op. cit.*, p. 3.
7. Ferling, *op. cit.*, p. 30.
8. *Ibid.*, p. 110.
9. *Ibid.*, p. 213.
10. *Ibid.*, p. 215.
11. C. Robbins, *Honest Heretic: Joseph Priestley in America*, Proceedings of the Am. Phil. Soc., February 1962, p. 72.
12. Priestley, quoted in Haraszti, *op. cit.*, p. 281.
13. J.B. Ginsberg, *Priestley, Jefferson, and Adams: The Émigre and American Politics*, Bull. Hist. Chem., Vol. 30, No. 2, 2005, pp. 94–5.
14. Priestley, quoted in Haraszti, *op. cit.*, p. 281.
15. Ginsberg, *op. cit.*, p. 96.

16. *Ibid.*, p. 91.
17. Priestley, quoted in J. Graham, *The Emigration of Joseph Priestley to America*, p. 109.
18. Pickering, quoted in Graham, *op. cit.*, p. 123.
19. Adams, quoted in Ginsberg, *op. cit.*, p. 96.
20. Priestley, quoted in Ginsberg, *op. cit.*, p. 97.
21. Adams, quoted in Haraszti, *op. cit.*, p. 284
22. Adams, quoted in Ginsberg, *op. cit.*, pp. 92–3.
23. M.A. Jones, *The Limits of Liberty*, p. 90.
24. Jefferson, quoted in F.M. Brodie, *Thomas Jefferson: An Intimate History*, p. 370.
25. *Ibid.*, p. 370.
26. *Ibid.*, p. 448.
27. Jefferson, quoted in Ginsberg, *op. cit.*, p. 97.
28. *Ibid.*, p. 98.
29. Priestley, quoted in Ginsberg, *op. cit.*, p. 98.
30. *Ibid.*, pp. 97-9.
31. J. Jackson, *A World on Fire*, p. 333.

Chapter 13: Conclusion
1. Priestley, Letter to Franklin, 27 September 1779.
2. Priestley, quoted in A. Lincoln, *Some Political and Social Ideas of English Dissent*, p. 175.
3. Cobbett, quoted in Lincoln, *op. cit.*, p. 179.
4. Lindsey, quoted in Lincoln, *op. cit.*, p. 57.

Further Reading

General Books Covering the Period
Jackson, J., *A World on Fire*, Penguin Books, New York, 2005.
Plumb, J.H., *England in the Eighteenth Century*, Penguin Books, Harmondsworth, 1969.
Porter, R., *Enlightenment*, Penguin Books, London, 2001.
O'Brien, P.O., *Debate Aborted, 1789–91*, Pentland Press, Durham, 1996.
Uglow, J., *The Lunar Men*, Faber and Faber, London, 2002.

The Lives of . . .
Adams, John; Jefferson, Thomas; and Washington, George
  Brodie, F.M., *Thomas Jefferson: An Intimate History*, Norton, New York, 1974.
  Ferlin, J., *Adams vs. Jefferson*, Oxford University Press, 2004.
  Ginsberg, J.B., *Priestley, Jefferson, and Adams: The Émigré and American Politics*, Bull. Hist. Chem., Vol. 30, No. 2, 2005.
  McCullough, D., *John Adams*, Simon and Schuster, New York, 2001.
  Vidal, G., *Inventing a Nation: Washington, Adams, Jefferson*, Yale University Press, New Haven, 2003.
Barbauld, Anna
  Aikin, L., *The Works of Mrs Barbauld*, 1825.
  Wakefield, D., *Anna Laetitia Barbauld*, Centaur Press, London, 2001.
Burke, Edmund
  Cobban, A., *Edmund Burke and the Revolt against the Eighteenth Century*, Allen and Unwin, London, 1960.
Cooper, Thomas
  Cohen, S.S., *Two Refugee Chemists in the United States, 1794*, Proc. Am. Phil. Soc., 1982.
  Malone, D., *The Public Life of Thomas Cooper*, Yale University Press, New Haven, 1926.
Cobbett, William
  Cole, G.D.H., *The Life of William Cobbett*, Collins, London, 1924.
  Ingrams, R., *William Cobbett*, Harper Collins, London, 2005.
Franklin, Benjamin
  Middlekauff, R., *Benjamin Franklin and his Enemies*, University of California Press, Berkeley, 1996.
  Van Doren, C., *Benjamin Franklin*, Viking Press, New York, 1938.
Horsley, Samuel
  Mather, F.C., *High Church Prophet: Bishop Samuel Horsley (1783–1806) and the Caroline Tradition in the Later Georgian Church*, Clarendon Press, Oxford, 1992.
King George III
  Griffith Davies, J.D., *George the Third*, Nicholson and Watson, London, 1936.
Lindsey, Theophilus
  Belsham, T., *Memoirs of Theophilus Lindsey*, Williams and Norgate, London, 1873.

Ditchfield, G.M., *Joseph Priestley and Theophilus Lindsey*, Trans. Unitarian Hist. Soc., April 2004.

Lavoisier, Antoine

Aykroyd, W.R., *Three Philosophers (Lavoisier, Priestley and Cavendish)*, Heinemann, London, 1935.

French, S.J., *Torch and Crucible: The Life and Death of Antoine Lavoisier*, Princeton University Press, 1941.

Pitt, William

Ehrman, J., *The Younger Pitt*, Constable, London, 1996.

Price, Richard

Cone, C.B., *Torchbearer of Freedom: The Influence of Richard Price on Eighteenth Century Thought*, Lexington, 1952.

Thomas, D.O., *The Honest Mind*, Oxford University Press, Oxford, 1977.

Priestley, Joseph

Beale, N., *Joseph Priestley in Calne*, Hobnob Press, 2008.

Bowers, J.D., *Joseph Priestley and English Unitarianism in America*, Pennsylvania State University Press, 2007.

Gibbs, F.W., *Joseph Priestley, Adventurer in Science and Champion of Truth*, Thomas Nelson, London, 1965.

Graham, J., *Revolutionary in Exile, the Emigration of Joseph Priestley to America, 1794–1804*, Am. Phil. Soc., Philadelphia, 1995.

Priestley, J., *Autobiography*, Adams and Dart, Bath, 1970.

Rutt, J.T. (ed.), *The Theological and Miscellaneous Works of Joseph Priestley*, London 1817–31, Parts 1 and 2: *Life and Correspondence*.

Wilkinson, John

Davies, R., *John Wilkinson, Ironmaster Extraordinary*, Broseley Local History Society, Nordley, 2001.

Soldon, N.C., *John Wilkinson (1728–1808), English Ironmaster and Inventor*, Edwin Mellen Press, Lewiston, 1998.

Index

The names and relevant chapters of the main characters of the book are in **bold** typeface. However, detailed page references to them and to Joseph Priestley are excluded because of their extensive appearance throughout.

Académie des Sciences 19, 25, 75, 78, 81, 83
Adams, Abigail 142, 143, 145
Adams, John – Chapter 12
Adams, John Quincy 144
Aikin, Anna, *see* **Anna Barbauld**
Aikin, John 53, 54, 56, 58, 59, 61, 62
Alien and Sedition Acts 131, 140, 144, 147, 148, 149
American Constitution 14, 24, 140, 143
American Revolution 14, 21, 22, 28, 31, 35, 41, 109, 119, 125, 140, 144, 156, 163, 164
Anti-Federalists (Jeffersonian Republicans) 103, 127
Arianism 6, 33

Banks, Joseph 88, 89, 98
Barbauld, Anna – Chapter 5
Barbauld, Rochemont 55, 56, 59, 61, 62
Batley Grammar School 5
Bayes, Thomas 30, 31, 39
Belsham, Thomas 92
Bentham, Jeremy 32, 35
Bersham ironworks 43, 44, 49
Biography, Chart of 6
Birmingham, Constitutional Society 11
Birmingham, New Meeting House Chapel *see* Meeting House, Birmingham
Birmingham, riots 12, 47, 50, 60, 61, 70, 99, 110, 116, 122, 128, 145, 163
Birstall 5
Blackburne, Francis 65–8
Blake, William 3
Blundell, Sarah *see* Sarah Price
Boulton, Matthew 43, 46, 50
Bowood Group 32
Bowood House 9, 24, 32, 57, 76, 158

Bradley ironworks 44, 48
Burke, Edmund – Chapter 10
Burke, Jane 119

Calne *see* Bowood House
Calvinism 5, 28, 33, 142, 143
Canton, John 18, 19, 32
Church of England, Thirty Nine Articles of *see* Thirty Nine
Club of Honest Whigs 18, 32
Cobbett, Anne 126, 134
Cobbett, William – Chapter 11
Constitutional Societies 116, 117
Cooper, Alice 97, 104
Cooper, Elizabeth 105
Cooper, Thomas – Chapter 9
Copley Medal (of the Royal Society) 18, 19
Custis, Martha *see* Martha Washington

Daventry Academy 5, 6
Declaration of Independence 3, 14, 22, 142, 149
Denman, Thomas Lord 56
Dephlogisticated air 10, 76, 77, 79, 81
Determinism 34
Dickinson College 104
Disquisitions relating to Matter and Spirit 33

Eames, John 29
Eighteen Hundred and Eleven 62, 164
Ellsworth, Hannah *see* Hannah Lindsey
Essay on the First Principles of Government 8, 21, 198
Essay towards solving a Problem in the Doctrine of Chances 30

Essex Street Unitarian Chapel 8, 68–72, 95
Experiments and Observations on Different Kinds of Air 79

Feathers' Tavern Petition 65, 66, 90
Federalists 103, 104, 129, 144, 146, 150
Free Discussion of the Doctrines of Materialism and Philosophical Necessity 34
Free will 33, 34
First Principles of Civil Government 98
Fitzroy, Augustus, Duke of Grafton 71
Fox, Charles 112, 113, 118
Franklin, Benjamin – Chapter 2
Franklin, Deborah 17
French National Convention 12
French Revolution 3, 11, 28, 35, 36, 41, 47, 52, 63, 75, 83, 93, 94, 99, 108, 109, 110, 112, 114, 115, 118–20, 122, 123, 128, 135, 146, 150, 156, 157, 159, 161–3

Gales, Joseph 116
George III, King – Chapter 10
Gibbon, Edward 90, 119
Greenwood, Alice *see* Alice Cooper

Hackney, New College 12, 61
Hemming, Elizabeth *see* Elizabeth Cooper
Historical View of Unitarianism 69
History and Present State of Electricity 7, 19, 21, 32
History of Early Opinions concerning Jesus Christ 10
History of the Corruptions of Christianity 10, 89, 90, 109, 153
Horsley, Mary 87
Horsley, Samuel – Chapter 8
Horsley, Sarah 94
Howard, John 28
Hymns in Prose for Children 58, 59

Industrial Revolution 2, 10, 41, 44, 46, 97, 126, 133, 156
Ingen Housz, Jan 162
Institutes of Natural and Revealed Religion 8

Jebb, Heneage Horsley 92
Jefferson, Martha 150
Jefferson, Thomas – Chapter 12
Johnson, Samuel 4, 33, 58, 161

Keighley, Sara 5
Kite experiment 20, 21

Lavoisier, Antoine – Chapter 7
Lavoisier, Marie-Anne 24, 74, 75, 78, 84
Leeds 5, 8, 53, 54, 65, 66, 113, 163
Leeds Library 8
Letters to the Inhabitants of Northumberland 132, 148, 154
Letters to the Right Honourable Edmund Burke 37
Lewis, Ann 42
Lindsey, Theophilus – Chapter 6
Lindsey, Hannah 66, 68
Locke, John 98
Louis XVI 93, 110, 122
Lunar Society 2, 10, 46, 81, 158

Manchester Constitutional Party 99
Manchester Herald 100
Manchester Literary and Philosophical Society 97, 99
Materialism 33, 34
Meeting House, Birmingham 10, 46, 70, 108
Memoir on Combustion in General 81
Mercuric oxide 76, 79
Méthode de Nomenclature Chimique 82
Methodism 4, 67, 90
Mill Hill Chapel, Leeds 8, 66
Monticello 150–2
Mount Vernon 138, 139
Mrs Silence Dogwood 17

Nantwich 6, 43
Needham Market 6
New Chemistry 80–4, 162
New York 13, 124, 125
Newton, Isaac 17, 85, 87, 88
Nicea, Council of 90, 91

Northumberland, Duke of 8, 65
Northumberland Gazette 103
Northumberland, Pennsylvania 12, 101, 102, 104, 154
Nugent, Jane *see* Jane Burke

Observations on the Emigration of Dr Joseph Priestley 127, 128, 129
Observations on the Nature of Civil Liberty and Policy of the War with America 34, 35
Oxygen 9, 10, 73, 76, 79, 80, 81, 84

Paine, Thomas 12, 38, 116, 120, 138, 139
Palgrave school 56, 59
Paulze, Marie-Anne *see* Marie-Anne Lavoisier
Peacefield 145
Pennsylvania Gazette 17, 21
Peter Porcupine *see* **William Cobbett**
Phlogiston 76, 77, 81, 83, 162
Pickering, Thomas 147, 148
Pitt, William, the younger – Chapter 10
Political Register 133, 134
Poor Richard's Almanac 15–17, 162
Porcupine's Gazette 129, 131
Price, Richard – Chapter 3
Price, Sarah 29, 46
Priestley, Henry 10, 11, 100
Priestley, Joseph, Jnr 8, 100
Priestley, Mary 6, 12, 43, 45, 53, 61, 63
Priestley, Sally 7, 60, 61
Priestley, William 8, 124

Quincy, Josiah 165

Rational Dissenters 3, 18, 33, 108, 162
Read, Deborah *see* Deborah Franklin
Reflections on the Revolution in France 11, 36, 47, 120, 121, 159
Review of the Principal Questions of Morals 29
Roman Catholicism 4, 58, 87, 110, 119, 160
Romantic Movement 4, 52, 63
Romilly, Samuel 32

Royal Society of London 7, 17, 19, 28, 30, 87, 98, 158
Rural Rides 133

Scheele, Carl Wilhelm 74, 80, 84
Scientific Revolution 2, 156
Shelburne, Earl of 9, 10, 28, 32, 46, 76, 77, 108, 110, 158, 162
Skelton, Martha *see* Martha Jefferson
Smith, Abigail *see* Abigail Adams
Some Information Respecting America 100
South Carolina College 105, 106
Stone, John Hurford 131, 148
Susquehanna River 100, 101

Tenter Abbey Academy 29
Test and Corporation Acts 3, 10, 60, 63, 67, 89, 98, 113, 114, 119, 158
Thirty Nine Articles 4, 65, 90, 97
Traite Elémentaire de Chemie 79
Trinity, doctrine of 8, 69, 90, 91, 92

Unitarianism 8, 89, 90, 92, 102, 162
University of Pennsylvania 104
University of South Carolina 105, 106
University of Virginia 154

Walker, Thomas 99, 100
Warrington Academy 6, 7, 18, 52–6, 61
Washington, George – Chapter 12
Washington, Martha 137
Watt, James 1, 10, 43, 46, 50, 99
Wedgewood, Josiah 10, 98
Wesley, John 3, 34
Wilberforce, William 60
Wilkinson, Ann (John's first wife) 43
Wilkinson, Isaac 42, 43
Wilkinson, John – Chapter 4
Wilkinson, Mary (wife of John) 42, 44
Wilkinson, Mary (sister of John) *see* Mary Priestley
Wilkinson, William (brother to John and Mary) 6, 43, 47
Wollstonecraft, Mary 52, 119